IT'S BLOGGABLE!

Your Voice Absolutely Matters
(even if you don't think so)

blog·ga·ble, (blogg - able) /'blägəbəl/
The freedom to express oneself via written word, video, or podcast. The courage to help others impact lives. The opportunity to build a passive online income via a conversion- focused blog.

Ewell Smith

Let's see what's possible!

Turn the page...

First addition published February 2021 Smith Press

ISBN: 978-0-578-79488-4

For information on bulk purchases, contact the author at https://ewellsmith.com/Contact

"The human voice is the most perfect instrument of all."

Arvo Pärt

Acknowledgements

Special thanks to my wife Jenny, whom I drive crazy with my ideas. She's the love of my life. She never stops challenging me to be better and inspires me every single day. Thank you to my parents Elaine and Ewell T, who endured my ADHD (God bless them) from early childhood on and who always support and encourage me. I love them dearly.

"Yesterday is history,
tomorrow a mystery,
and today is a gift. That
is why they call it the
present."

Author unknown

Contents

Forward

Ewell and I have been friends for a long time.

I've seen him thrive and struggle.

But I've never seen him give up.

You might say he's become a master of messaging through trial by fire.

During his time leading the Louisiana Seafood Promotion and Marketing Board, he guided commercial fishermen across Louisiana and the Gulf Coast to recovery through two of our nation's massive crisis events, Hurricane Katrina and the BP oil spill.

The fishermen were brought to their knees twice. I witnessed up-close Ewell and his team lead the way, saving such a rich culture that goes back six and seven generations.

Along the way, his ability to connect with people in every walk of life from media, his blogs, and TV to on- stage presentations has been masterful.

Ewell is a man of integrity. I know he put his all into this book for you.

Learn from him.
Be guided by him.
Be inspired by him.

But....

Most importantly follow his example.

What you're holding in your hands is a guide to connect to people.

It's a guide to get you going and keep going, especially now.

Don't just read this book.

Implement it on a daily basis.

And when you do, you will be connecting with your followers in such a deep way that you can and will change their lives forever.

I'm looking forward to reading your blog!

John Rowley
America's Lifestyle Strategist,
bestselling author

P.S. This book goes beyond blogging. It's life changing for you and for those you reach as it helps you find your voice.

“A crisis creates the opportunity to dip deep into the reservoirs of our very being, to rise to levels of confidence, strength, and resolve that otherwise we didn't think we possessed.”

Jon M. Huntsman Sr.

Preface

Your blogging journey starts here.

How in the world is it that you're here at this very moment?

You're here because of 12 food bloggers!

Before we jump into what you need to know to start your own blog, let me share a snapshot of my blogging journey with you...it started out a little rough.

In 2005, the historic and catastrophic Hurricane Katrina flipped our lives upside down in New Orleans, especially our fishing communities across coastal Louisiana. Katrina was a disastrous hurricane that caused more than 1,800 deaths and $125 billion in damage, one of the costliest hurricanes on record.

Our fishermen took the brunt of Katrina, losing everything, their homes, boats, trucks, fishing gear – everything. Some lost loved ones. Entire communities were literally wiped off the face of the earth; what was left was unrecognizable as major landmarks were gone.

At the time, I was living in New Orleans and leading the Louisiana Seafood Promotion and Marketing

Board. We were tested to the limits as we helped our fishermen recover. Through this process, we became master storytellers working with the media, and helping to rebuild our communities and restore billions of dollars in lost seafood sales.

After an absolutely exhausting and emotional five-year post-hurricane recovery run, Drew Brees and the New Orleans Saints took us to Superbowl XLIV on February 7, 2010. America cheered us on. And we won! It was the first Superbowl win ever for the New Orleans Saints. And the timing could not have been more perfect as the state of Louisiana needed renewed hope. As Drew held up the Superbowl trophy with confetti falling, I knew in that very moment we were back as a state. Our fishermen were back too.

Two months later, on April 20, 2010, our fishermen were blindsided by another disaster, the Deepwater Horizon oil rig explosion in the Gulf of Mexico that tragically took 11 lives and is now called one of the worst environmental disasters in United States' history.

Three days after the explosion, the oil rig sunk below the water line. From that moment on, it became known as the BP Oil Spill Crisis to our fishermen and to the world.

For 87 straight days, oil and methane gas spewed from an uncapped wellhead on the Deepwater Horizon, polluting the Gulf of Mexico.

The effects were widespread and devastating. Consumers across the United States were scared to eat our seafood because of the negative imagery from 24/7 wall-to-wall coverage of the black oil spilling into the waters. There were signs in restaurants and at food festivals from Chicago to Washington, DC to New York City reading, "We don't serve Gulf Seafood."

As a result, 98% percent of the Louisiana seafood markets disappeared globally. Our fishermen lost hope, and billions in seafood sales were lost, again, just like with Hurricane Katrina.

Once our seafood was deemed safe, we knew that we had to apply the lessons learned from Katrina and amp up our recovery efforts. What was different this time? Social media. Photos of those negative signs in the restaurant windows and videos of the media coverage were posted all over Facebook and Twitter. It would take more than the traditional PR strategies to restore the consumer's trust in our seafood.

This time, we saw a potential bright spot. Food bloggers! So we took a chance and flew in a dozen bloggers from across the United States to New Orleans. Are you ready for what happened next?

The food bloggers voices starting shifting the negative mindsets!

When the bloggers received the surprise calls from us, we didn't have to twist their arms to come to New Orleans for a week. They're natural adventurers!

During the days, we toured them to our fishing docks and seafood processors. And in the evenings, the catch from their crabbing, fishing, shrimping, and crawfishing day trips were turned into incredible 5-star dining experiences by New Orleans' award-winning chefs.

We treated the 12 food bloggers like rock stars.

As we worked with them, I realized how much I related to their passion for serving others and the creative spirit ignited by their blogs. It was these qualities that easily led us to them as influencers from the beginning. The quality of content on their blogs provided genuine value.

Daily, my eyes were opened to the power that blogging can have on lives. Their perspective and their storytelling were very personal and engaging, and their ability to connect at a deeper level was evident. Our expensive trade association's website quickly took a backseat to their voices.

I was humbled by the millions of people reached through the amplification of the bloggers' voices. The blogs truly made a difference in customer perception of our seafood, significantly impacting the futures of our fishermen for the better.

They also had the freedom and flexibility to call their own shots. That one week with those 12 bloggers inspired me to start my own personal blog!

Now let me start you off with this important fact that will reveal itself as you and I walk though this together in ***It's Bloggable!*** No matter your background or skill level, every single blogger starts in the same exact spot when learning the basics.

Blogging is what I refer to as a great equalizer.

Regardless of your experience level or age, everyone has the same shot of success with their own blog. From high school students, to career professionals, to moms, to dads, to military veterans, there's no mold for a successful blogger other than passion and determination.

You can't predict your surprise.

When they started blogging, I seriously doubt the dozen food bloggers ever dreamed they would receive a surprise adventure to New Orleans and coastal Louisiana, especially at such a critical time for our seafood industry.

With work and effort, blogging can also bring you adventures and special surprises too, as well as personal benefits that you'll discover.

Beyond storytelling, we'll talk about setting up your blog to begin building an income online. **I sincerely believe when we blog and share our voices for the right reasons, in addition to exciting opportunities, the income will follow.** (You'll notice that I didn't lead with mentioning income. I wanted you to first understand the root of my passion for blogging.)

We'll review leveraging affiliate marketing to create a pathway to your own passive online income (POI), and setting up your blog for conversion to avoid the typical rookie blogger's utter frustrations.

The skills that I learned through blogging literally made it possible for me to write my very first book – this book! To be quite candid, writing a book always seemed like something others did.

Do you see what I was doing? I was selling myself short. Our voices, whether through blogging or a book, further facilitate a stronger human connection that we all need now more than ever. Like our 12 food bloggers, our voices can literally transform lives.

Welcome to ***It's Bloggable!***

Let's see what's possible for you!

“The human voice is the organ of the soul.”

Henry Wadsworth Longfellow

Introduction

So you're thinking about starting a blog? That's exciting! Your new journey is about to begin so buckle up.

You may be feeling some frustrations right now about how to start; this is totally normal. Just don't let those feelings stop you! Too often, many aspiring bloggers quit before they ever really begin and don't benefit from the wealth of opportunities.

There's no need to second guess yourself. You're here for a larger reason, not for the technical things most blogging books rehash over and over.

It's Bloggable! will also help you avoid the costly rookie mistakes I made.

I certainly doubted myself during my blogging journey. **I doubted my own voice.** You don't have to doubt your voice **– you can take a different path.**

My desired outcome for ***It's Bloggable!*** is to help you realize that your voice is important and has value – even if you don't think so right now.

If you don't know what you want to blog about, that's ok. We'll explore what motivates you to start and keep blogging daily.

Let's ignite your interest and amplify it to feed your soul, your creativity, and your passion. Let's unleash your voice to make an impact.

To get you going, we're going to first address what I call **"Absolutely Mindset."** I define that as your through line from start to success. It's the connecting thread that binds your story together as you build upon your successes.

Your blogging through line is a seven-step journey that will reveal the most significant insights I learned from the dozen food bloggers in 2010.

Again, welcome to ***It's Bloggable!*** Let's see what's possible for you...

“A life is not important except in the impact it has on others lives.”

Jackie Robinson
MLB Player

Chapter One

Step 1: Understanding what your blog really means to you.

Everything points back to your blog.

The emails point back to your blog. The Facebook ads point back to your blog. Your Twitter feed points back to your blog. Your Instagram points back to your blog. Your LinkedIn posts point back to your blog. Your Pinterest points back to your blog. Your YouTube channel points back to your blog. The flyer you post at the local coffee shop points back to your blog. Your blog connects all your platforms and drives your sales!

A blog that is written and executed effectively is often the glue that pulls everything together for the online entrepreneur or the traditional business owner to communicate to the general public. **Your blog is your hub for inbound and outbound communications.**

By far, the most valuable assets you will use for your traditional business or for your online business are:

- Your blog.

- Your email list.

While more traditional and fancy websites are becoming online relics for businesses, the savvier business owners have clued into what solo entrepreneurial bloggers understood a long time ago. More traditional businessowners who understand are now leading the way with "conversion-focused blogs." These blogs are not static brochures. They are blogs that actually help you sell products and services that help others. The magic sauce is using email to leverage your blog to cultivate relationships over time with your community.

Simply put, blogs that harness the power of email are amazing storytelling platforms to drive sales, educate, build community, and create memberships.

At the end of the day, blogs that provide genuine value and help people solve their problems are more important now than ever before.

Now, let's see what's possible for you! Welcome to ***It's Bloggable!***

Here are a few key questions to ask yourself as we get started:

- Why is having my own blog such an important tool when leveraged correctly?

- How do I amplify my voice through blogging?

- What does blogging mean to me or my product's brand?

- How can blogging increase my personal income?

- What will blogging do for me personally?

What's your mindset?

Blogging starts with having what I refer to as "**Absolutely Mindset**." *That's your through* line *from start to success.*

I want you to think of your blog as your "online stage" for just a moment.

Now forget about the blog for a second. Think about stepping out from behind the curtain of a live concert stage of a packed arena and walking up to a "hot" microphone. You're about to address a crowd of 12,759 people.

For some of you, that's an adrenalin rush. For others, it may be shear panic and sweating palms. Stick with me. As you walk out, you can feel the heat of the spotlight as it shines down on just you. You can sense the audience eagerly looking up to you. You can feel the energy in the room!

The audience may have no idea who you are as you step out on that stage**. The key is that you have instant credibility the moment you speak into the microphone**. You can hear your voice reverberate on the rafters. If you were to tell the audience to sit down or stand up in that very moment, they likely would follow your instructions.

Now visualize 12,759 people standing up because you simply suggested they stand. They hear you. That's the power a well-executed blog gives you on the internet!

Your blog is a lot like your own online stage. As you provide genuine value, you become the authority in your space over time as you speak via the written word, podcast, or with video.

With that power comes the responsibility of serving and providing your audience with real value.

Let me repeat that.

With that power comes the responsibility of serving and providing your audience with real value.

Your audience may be zero or just a few dozen as you get going. That's ok. **Everyone starts in that exact same place.** Everyone faces that reality.

If you take blogging seriously, providing genuine consistent value while leveraging a conversion-focused blog, you can grow your online community from hundreds to thousands in time. Some grow their community to hundreds of thousands. As your community grows, your opportunities grow.

Also know this: you don't need hundreds of thousands in your community for success. You want to build a loyal base. Focus on that. Creating loyal followers happens as you provide genuine value. And, as that occurs, you start building upon the small wins to the bigger wins. Success builds.

If you're new to setting up a blog or looking to leverage your existing "hobby blog" that doesn't pay you, I want to put you in the right frame of mind. I know that may seem so obvious, but many people start with unrealistic expectations and slip into pitfalls when setting up a blog. I did that. You don't have to. You can start on the right path.

It's Bloggable! is the result of how I went from a hobby blogger to a conversion-focused blogger. Moving to this type of platform requires a mindset change. You can do this for sure.

You're reading this book as a result of that transition. Let's leverage your blog because your voice absolutely matters.

Let me share one more way to look at your blog that will carry over into every area of your life.

Again, we start with your **Absolutely Mindset**. The next most valuable asset you have in life and in business is your time. The most valuable skill you have is the ability to communicate well, really well to leverage your voice. That skill helps you further leverage your most valuable asset, your time.

The better you communicate, the more success you will have across the board. Your personal and business relationships will be stronger. You can make more sales. Serve more people. Buy back your time. Make more money to help your church, your family, your other business ventures, etc. At the end of the day, you can impact more lives.

Your blog is your own personal self-development tool that will help you network and sharpen your communications skills in written, audio, visual, or a combination of formats. I want you to look at your blog in that light going forward. Your blog is your very own personal self-development tool.

Your blog executed successfully will separate you from the pack immediately. It's a tool the majority of your peers simply do not have.

Cut yourself some slack as you sharpen your skills.

If you stumble like I did when I starting blogging – that's ok. I made plenty of missteps.

Give yourself permission to make mistakes. As long as you're taking action, recalibrating your mistakes, and moving forward, you're good.

The more you practice with your blog, just like with anything else, you will get better at it.

Your blog just happens to be your own public-facing platform to help you become an excellent communicator, which will help you in all areas of business and life. One human connection will naturally lead to another and then another, opening doors of opportunities.

Your blog is an *investment in yourself to gain skills to better serve others*.

Your blog is needed.

If you plan on doing business of any kind at any point in your life, you need your own blog. It may be a personal blog to build your personal brand or a business blog to support a more traditional business or your online business.

Many of us likely assume most existing traditional small businesses have an online presence of some sort.

That's not the case, at all.

Simply Google any small business segment, and you'll find established businesses that have yet to set up an online presence. Surprisingly and, not so surprisingly, some have yet to even start using social media, leaving a lot of business opportunities on the table.

To this day, I consult and work with nonprofit trade associations that represent small businesses. There are still some associations that are literally just getting started with their social media presence. It's also surprisingly common to come across trade association websites that are very dated and near extinct. The same can be said for many of their members' websites.

For those entrepreneurs and small businesses that provide genuine value and have an online presence and have mastered their blog to engage visitors to build relationships and drive leads, they're the ones leading their markets.

Two Important mindsets to reinforce:

1. A "pretty blog" is not your goal.

Having a "pretty blog" does not serve you at all if your blog is not helping you convert. A nice-looking blog helps for sure; however, your ability to convert sales is your goal.

Your blog must also be on a responsive platform. This means it is optimized and functions correctly on a smart phone, tablet, and computer screen.

2. You are the solution to someone's problem.

You have the answers to someone's question. The better you communicate with them online and offline, the more opportunities you will have to help and to serve them.

Let me ask you, what's the very first thing you do today when you need help with a problem or want to learn about a product or service?

You're likely picking up your cell phone to start searching for the answer. The person or business with the best online presence in their industry will get the first shot at helping you with a problem and providing you with a solution.

Your passive online income (POI) will be directly proportional to the value you offer on your blog and your ability to communicate an offer effectively.

Chapter Bonus: Two social media pitfalls for you to avoid

Many people are using Facebook, Twitter, Instagram, or LinkedIn as their **primary platform(s)** to build authority. That's risky for two reasons:

First, social media can create clutter, resulting in your key messages getting lost. There's no doubt the social platforms can be and are a powerful tool. But, candidly, your blog does something the social channels can't do.

Your blog eliminates all the clutter competing with cute cat videos and political rants on the social channels. You can laser focus the visitor's attention on your product or service when they are on your own platform. There are no rabbit holes or distractions for your visitors to chase after they land on your page.

Second, you don't own the social media platforms. Without owning your own platform, you run the risk of investing loads of time and resources into social platforms that can and will change the rules, algorithms, etc. any time they want.

We're seeing that happen more and more in real time. Also, some platforms have failed us by not keeping our data safe.

Social channels have a crucial role for sure. They are very powerful tools when leveraged to complement your conversion-focused blog. They further magnify your voice.

"He gives power to the faint, and to him who has no might he increases strength."

Isaiah 40:29

Chapter Two

Step 2: Determining if you are qualified to blog.

"Am I qualified to blog?" That's the question, it seems, we all ask ourselves at the outset. This goes to the root of having an Absolutely Mindset.

Let me address this issue right up front.

I believe the answer for you is: *yes, if you want to be*.

At the end of the day, it's what *you* believe, not me. Let's explore this further as we position you ahead of the pack...

Leverage the **"Step-Ahead" Theory.**

If you're learning a new skill and know just a tad bit more than another person, you can then share with others what you know. You're what I refer to as a Step Ahead!

If you have a few successes under your belt specific to your skill or knowledge, you can then share what you have learned. You're a *step ahead*!

It's as simple as that. You're an expert in the making.

Perhaps you have a high level of expertise on a particular subject or on "how to" do a certain activity. You have some solid real-world, tested successes. You're set to make a great impact.

You're an expert.

Even if you never start blogging, I want to paint a picture of the blatantly obvious that we often times miss: **the value of sharing or teaching others what you know helps both you and the other person more than you realize.**

Let me *simplistically* break this down with Jane's step-ahead story to make this crystal clear. I'll do this in a way that channels the fearless kid inside of each of us.

Jane is a Step - Ahead.

Jane and her good friend Johnny are in 10th grade. Both students are taking Algebra class. Jane and her entrepreneurial kid spirit sees an opportunity. She wants to tutor the kids in 9th grade pre-Algebra because she wants to earn a little spending money for some new outfits and going to the cinema on Saturday nights.

There are two things to notice here:

First, as a kid, Jane found her audience easily with the class literally behind hers. It was right there before her eyes. The other kids did not see the obvious.

Second, as a bonus, Jane may likely do better on her next Algebra exam because she has now taught what she has just learned. As she teaches the kids one grade behind her, Jane further sharpens her skills. All the while, Johnny simply consumes the same information.

Teaching becomes the most effective form of learning. Jane is now a step ahead of Johnny too! She's likely ahead of her entire class. This is what I call the Step-Ahead Theory.

Why I believe you can absolutely do this.

Your level of knowledge on a specific topic is dictated by your experiences and by your willingness to just dive in and learn new information. Just like Jane, the moment you begin sharing something that you've learned on your blog, you empower the group behind you. Your knowledge base grows with your experiences in life and through your blog. I know this sounds simple but it's also a fact.

Along this journey, bloggers who leverage their platform correctly and consistently provide content of genuine value become a recognized go-to expert.

> **Good bloggers get rewarded for *sharing* their knowledge while everyone else is focused on *consuming* the knowledge.**

The reward that bloggers receive is much more than just a financial reward. Blogging opens up doors of opportunity such as becoming a well-known speaker, book author, media consultant, or the go-to authority on a specific subject. And think about this:

Using your voice to impact lives may be your greatest opportunity of them all!

But what happens when self-sabotage creeps in? Here's a solution...

Self-sabotage is another significant hurdle we all face at some point blogging or in other areas of our lives. As we go along in our journey, we are our own toughest critic, doubting our abilities or our own value. You may ask, "Can I really do this?" Or, "Why should people care what I have to say?"

I've seen bloggers self-doubt with this particular question, "But am I certified or qualified to do this?"

This is super important to note: our fictional school kid, Jane, whom I mentioned above, was never certified!

We somehow tend to complicate simple things as we age. Then we procrastinate out of fear and/or discomfort, which is another form of self-sabotage.

Jane just did her thing. Like kids do. No fear.

In the real world, teachers have to attend school and train years to become a certified teacher.

This is the reality as a new blogger. We can take action the very moment we decide to.

Just the simple step of taking action starts to strip away self-doubt. Even in small steps, we will sense progress.

Progress builds confidence. Progress leads us to an **Absolutely Mindset**, the through line from start to success.

So, do what Jane does.

If you were to meet Jane, I believe our 10th grade entrepreneur-to-be would tell you in simple terms, while blowing a bubble, "your classroom of students is just behind you." And, many times, the classroom is now online, making your audience reach so much greater.

We learn by doing.

Here's another helpful example. I've been very fortunate to work with amazing chefs during my career promoting seafood with the Louisiana Seafood Board and as the producer of the Great American Seafood Cook-Off that aired on Food Network and PBS for years.

Some of the very best chefs I've worked with don't have a degree from a prestigious program like the CIA (Culinary Institute of America), which is an excellent program by the way. They developed their love for cooking and gained real-word experience by learning from their family.

Chef Cory Bahr from Monroe, Louisiana is a terrific example. Chef Bahr has no formal training. He learned how to cook from his grandmother.

He spent years next to her at the stove in her home. Then, like other great chefs, he had many chef mentors along his journey. This process of learning led him to championships at the Louisiana Seafood Cook-Off and on Food Network's "Chopped."

Along Chef Bahr's journey, he continues to share his culinary skills with dozens of chefs behind him in his own restaurants, giving back to the next generation. No doubt, Cory's grandmother taught him well.

Back to the question: Are you qualified to blog?

We can probably all agree, ***more so than we realize***:

- We all can be a little more self-aware of the knowledge, talents, and skills we can absolutely share to help others. *More so than we realize.*

- We need to know our voice matters to help change the lives of others. *More so than we realize.*

- We need to learn to cut ourselves a little slack. *More so than we realize.*

We're not going to be perfect as we get going. That's ok. The fact is, we'll get better as we start doing. This thought process leads us to an Absolutely Mindset.

Having a purpose larger than ourselves empowers us.

I strongly believe that you and I are put on this earth by God for a special purpose. Furthermore, every single one of us, including YOU, is a solution to another person's problems. Think about this, the human connection is rooted in this principle of us leaning on each other to help each other.

Serving others first to help them then helps us to shed our own fears and doubts even faster.

It’s simply in our DNA to help others.

So, can you do this?

Candidly, that's a question only you can answer. It starts and ends with your mindset. Be honest with yourself.

Blogging can be an amazing tool and a lot of fun if you choose to leverage it.

Chapter Note: A little common sense regarding blogging

Clearly, if you're going to be a lawyer, doctor, engineer, teacher, nurse, etc., your education, certificate, and licenses are absolutely needed like any field that's required by law.

But it is also important to note that **blogging fills in some essential gaps to solve real, everyday problems**.

For example, there are doctors and lawyers who blog who have created courses to teach college graduates how to take the MCAT to get into medical school or the LSAT to get into law school.

There are certified teachers blogging who have created courses to coach other teachers how to teach better and sell their pre-planned curriculums. Then we have students with their own blogs filling in the gaps the teachers miss.

At the end of the day, bloggers providing real value share practical, tested solutions to help others.

“Passion is energy. Feel the power that comes from focusing on what excites you.”

Oprah Winfrey

Chapter Three

Step 3: Considering what you should blog about.

To be truly successful on your blogging journey, let's focus on the areas you think you can serve others best. This is where you'll find genuine fulfillment.

Coming from a **mindset of serving others lays your foundation** to impact lives. In return, it will impact your life for the better. It's just the way that works.

I ask you, what are you passionate about?

When thinking about blogging, it's important to focus on those areas of genuine interest to you. Your authentic passion will always come across to those you aim to serve.

When your passion intersects with your knowledge base and/or skillset to help others, you've found your sweet spot.

Another important question for you to consider: Is there a market that will pay you for your idea, product, or service?

Here's a quick, two-step way to gain some insights to see if the market you're considering has a strong demand. You need to determine if the product or service you will provide is viable.

These steps, although non-scientific, can be very helpful in looking at the market:

Use “Google Trends” (https://trends.google.com)

to search areas of interest just as you would a normal Google search. You will be able to understand how often people are searching for certain terms or topics on Google. You can drill down to a specific location if needed. You will also be able to search different terms and compare them.

Using Google Trends, you will be able to determine the popularity of the product or service your blog will focus on.

2. Visit Facebook Ads Library (https://www.facebook.com/ads/library)

Once you learn what products or services are popular in Google Trends, you can gain a better understanding of what’s getting attention. You can do this by using Facebook Ads Library. You will be able to determine where the advertising dollars are going! You will also obtain a sense of how many people are advertising in that particular channel. That’s a very strong indicator for demand and passionate buyers.

There have been many blogs that started only with a person's hobby. Candidly, that may not be enough if your end goal is to build a business with your blog. Hobbies alone don't often pay well.

Many other bloggers have crossed the perfect intersection using their skills and passion to blog about a product or service that's in demand. That's your ideal spot you want to find yourself in.

So, what market are you considering to start?

Are you helping someone learn how to blog? Perhaps you're interested in teaching people through your blog how to pitch a baseball. Or pitch a new product or service. Maybe you're a handyman or handywoman that has a few tricks up your sleeve to fix common household problems. Or car problems. You may want to share with others how to overcome a broken relationship. Or an addiction. Or a loss of some kind. Or a weight issue. Perhaps you're a parent that knows how to home school children really well after home schooling your third child.

These topics are examples of what's bloggable. Why?

Because they solve real problems.

Someone wants to learn how to blog. Someone needs experienced guidance with their writing assignments. Someone needs to correct their curveball. Someone needs to learn the basics of cooking healthy meals for a diabetic family member. Someone has an awesome product or service to bring to market! Someone's crying from a broken heart.

I bet there's a parent out there wanting to know how to better home school their child right now as we function in this new coronavirus world. **I would further bet that person wants practical, real-world, tested and proven advice, not theory.**

That's what blogging of value does – it helps others solve real-world problems with real-world solutions.

What's possible for you?

Now let me share a really fun niche you might consider – would you be interested in blogging about succulents?

Yes, succulents! It's you. Perhaps the new you?

You're probably thinking, *this sounds crazy*.

Perhaps blogging about succulents is not what you were thinking, but let me show you what's possible.

Let me introduce you to Cassidy Tuttle.

When I first heard about Cassidy's blog Succulents and Sunshine, I was intrigued. She's been called the "Yoda of succulents."

So I Googled just the word "succulents" to see what would happen. Her blog popped up on the first page, organically.

When I saw her blog, I thought to myself, *it's the perfect example to show what's possible*. Her blog expertly helps others by sharing her experiences for something she herself was learning in real time.

But Cassidy's blog didn't start with succulents. By trade she was a professional photographer taking shots of her new subject, succulents.

She started with three succulents. She was simply trying to keep them alive on the windowsill of her basement apartment during the middle of winter in Utah. As she was learning how to care for succulents, she was photo journaling her progress on her photography blog. Over time, something interesting happened: her photography blog followers started paying more attention to the succulents' content than her other photography. In that moment, Succulents and Sunshine was born.

By default, Cassidy was sharing her photography skills and new knowledge on succulents in an incredibly friendly, very personal, and professional way.

One passion led to another. The connection of one audience helped her connect to and build another.

As Cassidy's new blog started positioning her as the authority on succulents, it then opened up a major door of opportunity for her. The publisher for *The Idiot's Guide* offered her a book deal. Her book *Idiot's Guide to Succulents* is now a bestseller on Amazon, which certainly helps to galvanize her credibility as the go-to expert on succulents. Her voice matters.

Cassidy teaches us:

- Anything is possible when done right
- You can teach what you're learning in real time (Step-Ahead Theory)
- A blog well done opens up doors of opportunity (*must be able to see and embrace*)

- There may be surprises along the way – sometimes a whole new exciting journey (*must be able to see and embrace*)

- A blog well done is non-threatening to a visitor, meaning a product or service can be recommended or presented in a positive way to create a passive income

- You can become an authority on a subject you love – your voice matters

Succulents are no doubt bloggable! Candidly, with an open mind and a little research, anything online is possible as evidenced by Cassidy and her blog. You never know where the journey will take you either...like Cassidy.

What's possible for you?

Chapter Bonus: Two traps to avoid regarding blogging

This is the reality: None of this is difficult to do but it will take effort and time on your part.

Sometimes, however, we can fall into one of two traps when setting up a blog.

The first trap is not seeking advice or failing to study what others have done before us. I did that!

Out of excitement, I simply jumped in head first with zero guidance using a freebie website service. Conversion wasn't even a word in my vocabulary when I started. My blog was only a hobby.

The second trap is researching something to death. This trap is the extreme opposite of the first one! There's an endless supply of good and bad blogging advice online and offline. I suggest finding one, two, or maybe three credible people to follow.

When you follow too many people, there is a good chance of falling into another trap. It's easy to become an information junkie. You may end up doing nothing. When people fall into this trap, *learning* is substituted for *doing*.

When you are at that point, learning becomes a tool to justify procrastination. It's comfortable. And comfortable is dangerous. It’s the exact opposite of Absolutely Mindset.

“I don’t care how much power, brilliance or energy you have, if you don’t harness it and focus it on a specific target, and hold it there you’re never going to accomplish as much as your ability warrants.”

Zig Ziglar

Chapter Four

Step 4: Laser-focusing your efforts to launch your blog.

Note – Three affiliate links are introduced in this chapter. In Chapter 6, I begin to explain why I'm sharing this note with you. I'll explain even further in Chapter 7 as we explore how bloggers can start monetizing their blog.

Now that you know you can start a blog, you may be asking yourself, "where do I begin?"

Starting your blog or online business correctly can be overwhelming without a clear path.

If you fight ADHD like me, there are many shiny objects to take you off course. We can get distracted. It's easy – too easy – to lose focus.

I lost focus and became confused while trying to write my first blog because I was concentrating on the overall process at once. I tried working on all parts of the blog at the same time. I was all over the place.

Something simple became complicated. I didn't feel like I was making any progress. I became very frustrated and developed self-doubt. To make my blog and especially this book a reality, I had to revisit some key lessons I learned early in life – all the way back in grade school.

A rude awakening

Mr. France, the school principal, told my mom when I was in kindergarten,

"Your son is incapable of learning."

I remember that day clear as a bell. My mom came to pick me up at the end of what was an ordinary school day for me. That meant me never sitting still. Getting out of my seat, walking around the classroom, and sometimes even walking out of the classroom while the teacher was teaching was normal. When mom arrived, Mr. France asked for a quick visit. I anxiously waited for my mom in the back seat of her deep blue 1970 Monte Carlo with the black vinyl top and black vinyl seats. It was hot outside that day, scorching hot with Louisiana humidity. Wearing shorts, my bare legs were sticking to the seats. Mom opened the car door then fell apart crying the moment she sat behind the steering wheel. I had no idea what had happened. She was devastated.

My mom didn't believe or didn't want to believe what the principal had told her. I'm so grateful she didn't give up on me. Mr. France did, however, instill enough fear and doubt in my mom to make her wonder, *What's wrong with my little boy*?

She made an appointment with a "special doctor," she told me. After a battery of testing, the psychiatrist told my mom, "your son *is* capable of learning. He's just a very hyperactive child. You need to be patient with him."

Today, that's called ADHD or Attention Deficit Hyperactivity Disorder.

Following a move to another school, my parents attempted to be "patient" with me. To say I tested my parent's nerves to the breaking point would be an understatement.

Frustration with learning was my theme. Back then, schools weren't trained to work with ADHD kids, implementing only traditional teaching methods. I couldn't understand why I had such a hard time learning simple things that my friends picked up almost immediately. I would study easily 3 to 5 hours a night for my good grades, while others studied maybe an hour.

ADHD also affected my love of sports. Sadly, I never stuck with a sport despite some natural abilities. I did, however, prove Mr. France wrong and my mom right to believe in me. I finished high school Magna Cum Laude with a 3.56 GPA. Deep down all of those years, I was driven by those kindergarten kid emotions from seeing my mom cry that day. Every once in a while, I reflect on this childhood memory and the missed opportunities for Mr. France to serve, to educate, to help my mom and me.

By the time I was graduating high school, college was the last thing I wanted to do. I was totally burned out on school, but once again, my parents refused to give up on me. I started LSU, promising to keep working and studying harder, but still not understanding the best way to learn or overcome ADHD.

Following in my dad's footsteps as a dentist, I enrolled as a pre-med student and graduated with a psychology degree. Quite a turn from where I started as a freshman.

Armed with a Bachelor of Science in psychology, I didn't feel prepared for anything in the workforce. So, the frustration only continued as I had no idea what I wanted to do with my life at that point.

After a few jobs, I defaulted to the one thing that was drilled into my head – school. This is going to sound crazy, and I know some of you will relate...it's all I knew. I went back to doing something I didn't enjoy at all to delay the reality of not knowing what to do. And I knew many people just like me going back to school since the job market was in a major decline at that time. I found some level of relief in knowing they were going back school too. Based on these circumstances, my plan seemed logical to me.

What do you love to do?

I didn't have an answer to this question for a long time, not until I met Jenny in grad school. Jenny started challenging me. She was the first person to ever ask me, "What do you love to do?" I froze. I couldn't answer her.

That question was the beginning of a new mindset and the process of healing for me. Over time, her question has resulted in a massive shift in the way I think and make decisions – and has helped me create a new lens for how I view everything around me.

After grad school, I started working with a publishing firm. It was during this season that I finally swallowed my foolish pride.

I was used to doing something I wasn't very passionate about. This was my story so far in life, and especially my education journey.

I accepted my new job for what I thought was "normal," to not enjoy work. That's so incredibly wrong. I was comfortable with the status quo. And, at the same time, knew I needed to make some changes in my life.

I first went to a psychiatrist (again, repeating behaviors) whose best solution was to prescribe me Ritalin on the second visit. She, in her mind, had me all figured out; just give me a pill. After a few months of taking that medication, I knew it wasn't the right thing for me. The prescription just made me a nervous wreck and incredibly anxious. It was a band aid, not a solution.

So I decided to seek out a new approach. I started thinking more about my passions and what I wanted to do in life. I found a counselor who led me through the process of how to not only manage ADHD but also leverage the creativity side of ADHD that was bottled up. I learned to stop blaming ADHD or my "attention issues" for my failures.

I started looking at ADHD as a blessing rather than a curse. That totally shifted my mindset. That was HUGE. I can't put down into words how life-changing this transition was for me.

By shifting my mindset, for the first time I could actually see how "chunking" a project down could help me. In psychology or linguistic analysis, chunking is grouping together connected items so that they can be stored or processed as single concepts. (Maybe my psychology degree is paying off at some level. Now that's funny!)

Interestingly, I had done it naturally through all those years of education as a survival method. Once I identified it and was able to actually label it, I continue to apply it to just about every area of my life and career with a renewed focus.

My new mindset propelled me into a new career, leading trade associations and representing some of America's hardest working people, commercial fishermen and loggers. I learned that I could use my core strengths and passions for marketing and PR to help people succeed with their vision. During this journey, the food bloggers I mentioned earlier inspired me to blog.

Learning to blog no doubt fueled my creative itch, while at the same time exposed my short attention span all over again but at deeper levels. Blogging reminded me very quickly I needed to chunk things down as I had learned over the years, while in school. Writing this book highlighted my ADHD tendencies yet again, but also reminded me that I can overcome by focusing and being disciplined.

If you struggle with focusing, I encourage you to test a simple method I'm about to show you. This effective method may work for you too be it blogging or any subject you're interested in tackling.

Clearly, this method is not rocket science as you will see. There's something I figured out about the simple process of writing down three important areas (or "rocks") to accomplish and stay focused on. This makes it possible to move forward and make progress.

My #1 hack to beat ADHD to launch my blog.

If I can hack my ADHD to launch my conversion-focused blog and write my very first book, ***It's Bloggable!***, you can too.

Have you heard the expression/question, "How do you eat an elephant?" It's cliché, I know. The answer is: "One bite at a time." And this is certainly true for starting your blog or taking on a new project.

The best way to do this is to set your overall goal and *"chunk it down"* into smaller digestible action steps that work for you.

I call it the **"Chunk It Down" Method.**

Three major rocks for you to focus on:

These rocks (think of them as stepping stones) are the basics you will need to start your blog (website).

This may seem a bit scary at first, but let me give you the steps and remove any hesitation you may be feeling.

Rock #1: Create a domain name and select a web hosting company

To create a domain name, first think of a domain that aligns with your products and services. Make sure it will be easy to remember for your readers and visitors.

One great strategy is to use your name (i.e. my main domain www.ewellsmith.com). The .com is most preferable because .com is so engrained in our culture. If your name is not available, you can get creative or use another suffix. My next choices would be .co for a profit venture or .gov for a nonprofit venture, because of their popularity.

Then, buy the domain name using a trusted company (Networksolutions and BlueHost are great choices and have great ratings).

Next, sign up with a web hosting company (I've used BlueHost for over five years) so you can launch your website once it's built. This is the company that will "host" your website on their servers.

Based on the web hosting company you choose, you may want to use your web hosting company to establish your professional email addresses also.

BlueHost offers a variety of services and tools that streamline this process. Aside from several years of very good service, one thing worth mentioning is they provide a free SSL Certificate that keeps your website visitor's information safe proving your site/blog is using an encrypted channel. That's the lock you see next to a domain name in the browser; if you don't see that lock on a site, it may not be safe. As you start paying attention to other websites – in this case checking to see if a particular site is secure, these are the subtle things that do make a difference. Not flashy, but important. No matter the service you work with, make your site is secure.

Learn more here about BlueHost:
www.ewellsmith.com/BlueHost

Rock #2. Select a good web building tool so you can build your blog

Using the web building software you choose, load a conversion-focused theme and start building your blog – a regularly updated website.

After much research, I chose Thrive Themes. The theme you choose provides your overall design and the conversion features that you'll be using to acquire more customers.

I highly recommend using Thrive Themes for Rock #2. Thrive Themes is an advanced but simple-to-use WordPress suite of website tools.

With Thrive Themes, you can easily create a conversion-focused blog on your website. This is important to know: I created my blog with zero tech skills. Like me, you'll be able to customize the theme to fit your personality, style, and subject matter. You can also build out as many pages as you'd like. I recommend no more than 5-6 pages at the start. Like BlueHost, I've used Thrive for several years.

Learn more here about Thrive Themes:
www.ewellsmith.com/Thrive

Rock #3: Set up your automated emails

It's time to start writing your emails and setting up your email service.

For my blog, I chose GetResponse because their automation sequence is very intuitive and so easy to use. It also helps me create a very organized email list and capture important data, including open rates, click rates, and forwards, to name just a few of the features.

You can learn more here:
www.ewellsmith.com/GetResponse

You may be asking, "What do I need to know about these emails and how do I set them up?" Great questions!

First, your emails are VERY important tools that you'll use to build a relationship and personal connection with your potential customers as you guide them on a meaningful journey.

AND it's where your sales conversions often happen!

So don't skip over this essential part of the process as you move forward with your blog.

Let's focus in on two very effective types of emails: nurturing emails and sales emails.

Nurturing emails (also called "drip campaigns" are ongoing email campaigns that "nurture" your relationship with a potential customer. What you're doing with these emails is "dripping" information about how you can add value to the potential customers' lives and help them solve their business problems with a proven solution.

Sales emails are a continuation of the nurturing process but the focus is on closing the deal. With the sales emails, you're able to focus more on the full story of how your products can help your customers. And, you can be more direct with your "ask" and challenge them to try your products.

How do you create these emails? Let's dive in:

My favorite source for learning how to write and structure both nurturing and sales emails is the *Marketing Made Simple* book by Donald Miller sold on Amazon.

In his book, he gives clear direction on how to create these emails. He points out that there is no magic number of emails in your email campaign. He says it's more about how to keep your customers engaged in your process, as you guide them along the way in their journey.

Donald Miller details how to create six effective, consecutive sales emails:

Email #1: Deliver the asset (Deliver the item you promised the customers when they clicked the button where you mentioned a free eBook, video, or consultation, for example.)

Email #2: Identify with their immediate problem and provide a proven solution

Email #3: Customer testimonial (These are always a win because they build instant credibility. And they're easy to get from a happy customer!)

Email #4: Overcome an objection (Your customer may be ready to buy but may have some kind of objection that you need to address with confidence, reminding them of your ideal solution for them.)

Email #5: Paradigm shift (Basically, you have to tell the customer, "You used to think this way, but now you should think this way.")

Email #6: Sales email (Only ask for the sale BUT without selling!)

After you have written your sales (and nurturing emails – *Marketing Made Simple* will show you how to create these too), you will move them into your ESP that I talked about above.

This is where a good, proven ESP will become your best friend. Many of them require no coding experience at all! You simply set up your six emails (or whatever number you feel is best for your target audience), and use the software to schedule them out. A few days between each email is a good rule of thumb.

Once your basic email auto responders are set up (this happens quickly), you can then build additional custom responses as you gain skills leveraging direct response email.

Remember, at this stage, your primary goal is to get going. Get the wins in and build on them.

These three "rocks" are the steps you'll need to start your blog.

Once you know "what" to do, it's time to clock it.

I like to use the phrase, **"Clock the rocks."**

Here's what I mean.

It's important to set up a "clock" or timeline for each "rock." Without any timelines, you can't drive forward effectively.

Between each rock, you need to establish some smaller rocks (i.e., reasonable timeframes) for accomplishing each part of the overall process.

Rock #1 can be accomplished pretty quickly. Rock #2 and #3 will take longer and require more time and effort.

Working against a timeline will definitely help you and ensure you get each task done. If you let the tasks float out there without deadlines, your project will do just that, float.

Every blogger and business owner that has gone before you and I have been exactly where you are right now. **You're not alone. We all deal with the mental gymnastics of how to get this done.**

Remember to "Chunk It Down." **This is exactly what I did to launch my blog.**

After learning what those before me have done really well, I took action. I still made mistakes. I then corrected those mistakes and continued to refine. And one of my areas of refinement was learning to "clock the rocks."

As you complete Rock #1, you will have momentum and positive energy to move to Rock #2 and Rock #3.

And once you have that momentum, your blog is absolutely more doable in your mind. You can mentally see progress as you work through your timeline on the smaller rocks. With the smaller rocks in place, your process just got easier. Why? Because you "chunked it down."

Let the "Chunk It Down" method work for you too!

I launched my new conversion-focused blog with only three tools to start. I used BlueHost, Thrive Themes, and GetResponse. That strategy worked really well for me. It made it possible for me to focus again. It helped me to eliminate all the distractions and rabbit trails the internet can take you down. Here are the links:

Rock 1. www.ewellsmith.com/BlueHost

Rock 2. www.ewellsmith.com/Thrive

Rock 3. www.ewellsmith.com/GetResponse

The only difficult part is actually getting started. Rock #1 is your **first mental step.** It's where your momentum first begins.

Stepping out on to Rock #1 is a big step of faith on your part. It's believing in yourself. It's simply putting one foot in front of the other. You can do it! You'll discover yourself saying, "I love to blog!"

“The best way to find yourself is to lose yourself in the service of others.”

Mahatma Gandhi

Chapter Five

Step 5: Setting up your Home Page and About Page correctly.

Genuine human connection is the intent of your Home Page and your About Page. For that reason, I make a deliberate call-out for both pages. I'll explain at the end of the chapter why; I want you to see the pattern first as a "common thread" that reveals itself. While I provide some helpful technical tips in this chapter that will serve you and your visitors well, you will see that this chapter is more about mindset.

We'll start with the Home Page

Have you ever landed on a home page and wondered what the site was actually about? You might (I use the word "might" loosely) click on something since you found the page and then leave that website. How many times have you done that? Plenty I suspect.

Let's drill down on why you leave a site quickly. Two reasons lead to the root cause:

1. The wording (communications) on that site was not engaging, or worse, it was confusing.

2. The layout to facilitate the communications was not engaging or had no hierarchy of importance and no clear structure.

If a website or blog does not quickly grab your attention, it doesn't even give you the opportunity to consider the offer.

When they don't make the offer blatantly obvious and easily understood immediately, they have no shot at helping you address your problem. That's the root issue. You then leave.

You have only a few seconds to capture a new visitor's attention to your blog to let them know you have a way to help them.

Avoid this "Trap"

Another trap is our natural tendency to make our Home Page about ourselves. Because we create it, we want to make it about our own story and success.

But your blog should really be about helping make the visitor's life better. You have to think of the visitor as the hero of the story. You are simply the guide to help the visitor in their journey.

I totally blew this on my hobby blog. I used my blog like a resume as I started out. I never once addressed the visitor in a way that said, "I'm here to help you." Rather, it became a way to only show off my projects end experiences. Sure, that may lend to some credibility perhaps, but what a missed opportunity.

Even as an experienced marketer and PR professional, I totally lost sight of my visitors' needs like so many other bloggers do. I was too close to it. And, candidly, I was too self-consumed with it. Many businesses often make the same mistake with their website or blog, which may look nice at first glance but doesn't engage the visitor.

This explains why people have a high "bounce rate" on their blog or on their business site. The bounce rate is the percentage of people who arrive to your blog and then leave (bounce) rather than continue on to other pages or respond to your call to action.

How do you fix this?

1. First you keep your focus on your visitor and how you may solve their problem. That mindset will help you to make sure you "offer" something of value to them.

2. Use the Z BILLBOARD format. This is so simple and it works. It's important to understand the most important locations on your home page to plant the most important messages or "calls to action."

Your eye and your visitors' eye will naturally scan a website's home page like a "Z."

An easy way to look at this is as one full computer screen page as the main part of the home page. It may be a little less than a full computer screen page. Some people use an old newspaper terminology to describe the top portion of the home page. They call it the "above the fold" portion. I refer to it as **the billboard** portion of your home page.

And just like a billboard along the interstate, you only have a second or two to connect with the reader before they pass by at 65mph, or in this case at the click of a mouse on your blog.

This is how our minds work...

Looking at the top of the blog's home page for the first time, from left to right you scan the menu bar, then your eye will cross over diagonally to the left bottom corner of the "billboard," then you scan again left to right horizontally.

The two most important parts on this billboard are the top right corner in the menu bar and the middle of the Z's spine.

When you visit a well-done blog, often times that top right menu button will be a different color and perhaps larger. That button is typically a "call to action" that brings the visitor to the next most important step for conversion. We will talk more about conversion in Chapter Six.

The top right corner is your first opportunity of having someone click on your site.

The next most important part of the billboard is directly in the middle as the visitor scans back down the spine of the Z across the middle. That's where your message goes with another call to action button. This is the part that helps the visitor understand what the blog is immediately about. It's what I refer to as your "title offer."

The underlying image may support your messaging or be a solid color. There are many ways this can all be designed to complement your message.

3. Use simple words. Use easy words. Use few words.

Your visitors won't read much copy, especially at the top of the page. Too many words or using long sentences will guarantee a high bounce rate. Remember, you've got maybe a second or two for your visitor to digest the home page and your offer. Easy words matter. Placement matters.

Now let's look at the "About Page"

You may have numerous professional credentials you like listing next to your name. You may have accomplished some prestigious things you want to mention up front. Save it so you don't waste a great opportunity here. Most bloggers screw up on this page.

The #1 mistake most bloggers make is making their "About Page" all about themselves, not their visitor. I know this seems to be so counter intuitive. That's why most mess this page up worse than they do the Home Page.

We can fix this issue so easily – just know it's truly not about you. There's a theme developing here...your blog's focus should be on serving others. When that's your focus, that's when your voice has the biggest impact. That's when you truly connect.

Your About Page will get traffic! To underestimate this humble page is a big mistake. Your About Page is so important and unique that it gets its own space in the menu bar.

Once people get to your site, curiosity kicks in. Your visitor will want to know a bit more about the person that makes the blog tick. That's you.

They will want to peek into your background which presents a great opportunity for you. So, let's put that traffic to good use for conversion. As a blogger, you have a unique opportunity to connect personally here with your visitors.

Setting up your "About Page" in 3 simple steps in the form of a personal letter.

Before we move into the 3 simple steps, imagine you are writing a brief, personal, emotionally warm letter to your friend.

Step 1. Address your visitor's problem up front and hint to how you may solve it. Agitate their problem by bringing up a relevant pain point they are struggling to solve.

Step 2. Empathize with your visitor (keep thinking of them as a friend) about the issue so you can help them with a proven solution. Let them know you "appreciate" and understand their situation. Let them know you've been in their shoes. Then share *some* of your story and background that will help them win and be the hero.

Your visitor does not need to know or want to know every detail of your life story here, just a glimpse of the portion of the story that will directly relate to them and help them. That's about all they care about at this stage.

If you do this part right, you'll build a relationship with your visitors over time and they will want to know the other details of your life. At the moment, however, the new visitor is on your site to first solve their own problem. And they want to know that you can help them solve their problem.

Step 3. Transition quickly back to your visitor, making your About Page work for you by making it about them. Share specifically how you can help them and paint a positive picture for them regarding their outcome.

What I like about this format is that your letter is personal. It's an opportunity to ask for your readers' email address to open a dialog with them. It leverages the conversion focused mindset so you can then continue the conversation.

How to use your story – briefly.

Everyone has a unique background or story that can be told to help others. Your personal story matters. It doesn't have to be totally unique or over the top. In fact, ordinary stories will connect with most people at an everyday level.

Your story simply needs to be candid. To the point. No need to embellish. Your story is what it is. That's what makes it authentic and relatable.

So you might be thinking your story is boring or you haven't had any major challenges (count your blessings) worth sharing to help others. If that's the case, that's ok.

This is what you do. Make being normal part of your story because many people in your audience are likely in the same boat as you are or once were.

Get creative and use it. Let me use my "starting out in life/career story" as my story and as an example for new bloggers.

I call it my **"Grey Cubical Cell" period** of my career, which was my starting point in my early 20s. I landed my first "real job" with a regional publishing firm. In short, they stuck me in the corner of a very large room filled with grey cubicles. As the new guy, my grey cubicle was tiny. That was absolutely mind numbing for me. I felt like I was crawling the walls. My voice was not heard at all.

I got my one and only ulcer in my life, literally, being cooped up in a tiny cubical with grey padded walls.

Not only did I feel confined in a tiny space, the work was very repetitive. I was bored out of my mind. The work they assigned me didn't tap into my creativity.

I was very grateful for the job starting out because I learned a ton and made some good friends. But I felt stuck. I felt trapped. My voice didn't seem to have an impact.

It was Jenny, my girlfriend, who recognized my frustrations and helped me find a way out.

She's the one who encouraged me to pursue my passion to get out the “grey cubical cell.” Up to that point, no one had ever asked me, "What do you love to do?" No one had ever challenged me to pursue my passions. Jenny did.

When I got the ulcer is when I knew I had had enough. Jenny’s words of encouragement came to life. At that moment is when I dedicated myself to pursuing a career that tapped into my creativity and passion for serving others.

That’s it. Then I would transition to the reader on guiding them how to get out of a situation one might feel stuck in like I was. I suspect a lot of folks are trapped in their own version of the “grey cubical cell” – literally. I image some feel like I did too where my voice didn’t seem relevant in that environment.

This is exactly why I would have shared that story – it was so real to me and so frustrating. I can see the stark contrast in my life today, loving what I've been able to do for 25 years and now blogging as a new passion. I know I'm very fortunate and never want to take my experience and opportunities for granted.

Do you know "The Why" part of your story?

Let me add this: your visitor is checking into your About Page because they're looking for reassurance you can help them. They also deep down want to know you actually care about helping them. They can sense that.

That's your "why." **Knowing your "why" matters because your visitors will recognize your genuine passion. The "why" lays the foundation for your blog.**

Before we wrap up this chapter, here's something else NOT to do. You'll see in just a second why I prefer using a letter format for the About Page.

If you want to put your visitors to sleep right away, writing your About Page in third person will do the trick.

There is nothing worse than this type of copy on a personal blog:

"Joe Brown was the Marketing Manager of XYZ company for 7 years. After losing his job, today Mr. Brown teaches people to bla, bla, bla, bla, bla. With a BA from the University of IDC in Florida (I don't care) and his Masters from University of IDC in DC, Mr. Brown can help you get more clients."

Snoooozzzz.

Candidly, most people suspect the blogger writes their own About Page. Your visitors know that. So, just be yourself. Use normal language that reflects you. People will see through the formality really quick.

Keep it real.

Use the word "I." (but not too much) Make it personal. Own it.

Pretend you're getting to know a friend and you're sharing your personal life stories and interests. The use of the first person "I" connects with your visitors on a personal level, which is critical. That bond creates trust. Trust is the foundation of your potential to impact lives and earn a passive online income over time.

If you already have an About Page written in 3rd person, I suggest revisiting your page and making it human and personal sounding. The last thing you want is to sound like a politician talking in 3rd person about herself or himself on an election brochure.

What if you already have an existing small business supported by your blog or website?

I would still consider making your About Page first person.

Small business is personal. It's why people love to support the people or families that own them compared to a large corporation with shareholders.

Simply use the same formula above telling a brief story of your business to establish credibility and quickly transition to how your business solves your customer's problem.

Then you may want to offer a free giveaway in return for an email address in a casual manner to get them engaged. Again, it's about them. It's not about you.

Let’s recap the About Page:

- Know your visitor is more important than you.

- Know your "why."

- Be you, in the first person.

- Tell your story briefly and transition from you to them, *quickly*.

- Invite your visitor to stay in touch with you in an authentic, conversational way to capture emails.

The “common thread” is not you.

It may be very apparent by now what the common thread is between the Home Page and the About Page. It’s a two-millimeter shift as Tony Robbins would say. This is absolutely about mindset – your mindset to set the proper tone or to create the right path to welcome and embrace your visitor's mind immediately. It’s all about your visitor and making a genuine connection.

As tempting as it is to make our blog about ourselves, the first impression on the Home Page is only a success if the messaging is crystal clear and it screams, “We’re here to solve problem X and help you succeed." That must happen in less than 1 second. Remember, you're communicating at the speed of a mouse click.

Your About Page must then back up your messaging on the Home Page. If you shift gears too hard making your About Page all about yourself after you successfully pull your visitor into your site, you just discredited your efforts on the Home Page.

At the end of the day, your through line from start to success with your blog is putting your visitors first. **It's about them, not you!** Keep that in mind throughout your blog and you will serve them well while building your community over time.

Chapter Bonus: Your P.S. matters

The Powerful P.S. If you were to look at my personal blog's About Page, https://ewellsmith.com/About/, you will notice my use of the P.S.

Following my signature, I leveraged one of the most effective writing tools you can use. The P.S.

Next to the first line of a letter, the P.S. is the second most-read content of any letter.

If you have a certain message or call to action you want to emphasize, make sure to include that in your P.S. Even though you've already stated your main message or call to action, it's always a best practice to restate them in your P.S. because, again, they will get read.

“When you make a mistake, admit it, correct it, and learn from it – immediately."

Stephen R. Covey

Chapter Six

Step 6: Discovering the 13 "hobby blogger" mistakes and learning to avoid them.

Buckle up as we go through the mistakes below that I made along the way. Mistake #13 made for a bumpy ride. Here's the good news: *after each mistake, I provide a tested solution to help you.*

*Note – I will introduce you to products and services below that I've used to build my personal blog the correct way. Because these are services I trust, I share their affiliate links. Should you decide to use their service, I earn a small commission at no added expense to you. **I'm going far above and beyond sharing this notice in a book to drive home an important point**. In the following chapter (Chapter 7), you will gain a greater understanding of why I'm sharing this with you upfront and how bloggers use affiliate marketing on their blogs and their Resources Page to build a passive online income (POI).*

Frustration defines the well-worn hobby blogger path.

None of these mistakes need to happen with you:

Hobby Blogger Mistake #1

Using a Free Blog Platform

You may have already heard about this. It's because this one mistake is repeated over and over and over by new bloggers. It costs them. **The freebie sites will lure you in, then upsell you to utilize some of the bells and whistles they offer. However, that's not the real cost I'm talking about. There are three real costs to be aware of:**

Cost #1. The limited ability to scale to your full potential. As your blog and audience grow, you'll find out quickly the limitations operating within the free service, even with the upsells they offer. You'll also realize that ***you do not own your blog, therefore, you do not have control.***

Cost #2. The extensive time required to move to a better blogging platform. Realizing this truth can be painful. It's like that feeling when you're writing an essay and your computer crashes, and you lose your essay. Starting over is never fun.

Cost #3. A limited skillset and knowledge base about blogging. These only come when you build and own your own blog. **This is the costliest of the three in my opinion.**

Like anything worthwhile, blogging takes effort on your part. With that effort you will gain new skills and knowledge through this process that are transferable to other areas of business and life. It's the edge we need as entrepreneurs knowing our business from the ground up.

The Blog Fix

Start with your own WordPress site.

WordPress allows you to choose from a wide range of themes to design your site and applications which are referred to as plugins or apps. These tools eliminate the frustration of being limited – you will now be able to scale your site that you own 100% to meet your needs as you grow.

To do this, I used BlueHost which made this easy. By going through BlueHost, you can actually set up a WordPress blog.

BlueHost is incredibly affordable and surprisingly quick, painless, and easy to launch. I've used them for over five years with excellent service. They have recently streamlined their process making it even better and faster to go live. BlueHost regularly runs special promotions for new users, see my link for their current offer: www.ewellsmith.com/BlueHost

Hobby Blogger Mistake #2

Zero Conversion Abilities

If your goal is to make an income with your blog, avoiding this mistake is key for you.

I never even heard the word conversion as it related to blogging when I started with a freebie site. It was never even a consideration. As I transitioned from the free site to a WordPress site, I was lured into making a "fancy WordPress blog with a pretty theme."

As basic as this was, my "fancy" WordPress blog had no built-in way to capture emails. I had zero conversion ability. I had no way to connect with others through my blog and no way to grow my online community. And keep this in mind: as your community grows, your opportunities grow.

Going in, this is the mindset needed: conversion is as important as owning your own blog. If you don't build in a way for conversion, there's no point in starting a blog, if your intention is to build a passive online income (POI).

The Conversion Fix

Pick a conversion-focused WordPress theme.

This means the theme is designed with the tools to make it easy to capture leads, to make your site run faster (by optimizing photos for example), to A/B test your titles, run quizzes, build sales funnels, build landing pages, and easily post testimonials. These are just some of the capabilities available.

As I mentioned earlier, I love Thrive Themes. All the tools and assets described above are built into Thrive Themes.

My first "pretty" WordPress theme had zero conversion tools built in. Thrive Themes has all the tools in I use and need, eliminating compatibility issues other external plugins cause.

Thrive Themes gave me the ability to:

1. Build my blog with **zero technical skills.**

2. Speed up the learning curve using their intuitive drag and drop design in real time.

This is my analogy which is very fitting and exactly how I feel about Thrive Themes. As easily as you use Microsoft Word for writing a paper, you can use WordPress with Thrive Themes to build your blog.

Learn more about why I love Thrive here:
www.ewellsmith.com/Thrive

Hobby Blogger Mistake #3

No Lead Magnet

Typically, a lead magnet (also called a lead generator) is a free product or service of value in exchange for your email.

The first thing this does it provide an opportunity to establish trust providing a value upfront for free.

Second, over time, a lead magnet provides the opportunity to get to know each other which then may present opportunities to further support each other.

Common lead magnets, listed in very strategic locations on your website, include items such as:

- Instructional videos
- Webinars
- Top 10 lists
- Discounted memberships
- e-Books
- Cheat sheets or checklists
- Templates
- Audio series
- Tool kits or resource lists
- Assessments
- Free consultations

I did not have a lead magnet on my freebie blog (that was not even an option on the free site), and I did not have one on my first “pretty” WordPress blog. And it wasn’t easy to fix this problem.

In short, who really knows how much this mistake actually cost me. This was a big mistake.

The Lead Magnet Fix

Find a conversion-focused WordPress theme.

Once again, finding a conversion-focused theme is the solution.

Something as easy as capturing email addresses was not built in with my first “pretty” theme. Thrive Themes makes this part very easy and coaches you how. I built my site with zero coding skills. Thrive Themes has one focus – conversion. That’s what I knew I needed when I started taking my blog seriously. See how easy it is to use Thrive to capture leads: www.ewellsmith.com/Thrive

Hobby Blogger Mistake #4

No Email Strategy

Early on, my so-called email strategy was limited to turning on the basic automated response to say "thank you for your email." The strategy fell off the cliff after that.

We've talked a good deal about capturing email addresses as part of your conversion strategy. There's a very good reason for this. Despite the perception of emails overwhelming people's email boxes, despite the myth "email is dead" and despite the email marketing channel shrinking some, the reality is **email is still the #1 way end-users want to be communicated with by far.**

Large corporations invest heavily in email for this reason. Email marketing to this day provides the best return dollar for dollar by far than any other marketing platform. For every $1 spent, they see on average a $44 return (source: Campaign Monitor).

Just like how the email strategy works for larger corporations, it also works for individual bloggers like you and me. It may even work better when done right because our ability as bloggers to connect at a personal level is much higher.

Think about this: 90% of email gets delivered to the intended recipient's inbox, whereas only 2% of your Facebook fans see your posts in their newsfeed without using paid promotion (source: Forrester Research). Email done right works.

Last note on the "email is dead" myth: As you study this space, you will see many marketers pushing direct Facebook ads to sell, leading you to believe that it's now the only way to effectively re-target. Yes, those tactics work exceptionally well when executed well. They're powerful. And guess what drives the sales once you're in their orbit? Email follow ups. And guess where they send you at some point. Likely to their blog.

Why is your email strategy so important?

Because you maintain control!

We see people investing enormous amounts of time and money on social channels to drive marketing. However, recently we've seen the shakeup on some social channels over security, changes in algorithms, etc.

This issue parallels why you want to own your blog. **Your email list is yours. Email has been the one constant for online communications and the consistent connection to the customer. Your email list to this day is still your most valuable marketing**

asset to complement your blog. Email drives your passive online income (POI) on your own blog.

The Email Strategy Fix

Find the right email service provider (ESP).

You want to create customized emails and well-thought-out sequences of automated responses as you grow into this.

After using another service for some really basic free and limited applications, I needed to step up and switched to GetResponse because their automation sequence is very intuitive and so easy to use. It also helps me create a very organized email list and capture important data, including open rates, click rates, and forwards, to name just a few of the features.

Learn more about GetResponse:
www.ewellsmith.com/GetResponse

Hobby Blogger Mistake #5

SEO Apathy

This misstep was not so much a mistake but more, "what the heck do I do regarding search engine optimization (SEO)?"

I knew it was important to have SEO but the first "freebie" site I had only allowed me to put a few keywords in a very specific field they provided. There was no real SEO strategy or research on my part, just selecting a few keywords.

I suspect you've likely heard about the importance of SEO to get your blog posts discovered. It may intimidate you. It does for many bloggers. It did for me, and I simply moved away from it. That was my mistake.

While SEO is very important, there's no need to get stressed out about this. Remember these two points:

SEO takes time to kick in. Just because you launch a site doesn't mean you will rank high on Google or other search engines right away. It takes time for SEO to gain traction.

Search engines change their algorithms all the time. Trying to keep up with algorithm changes is beyond the level needed to execute basic SEO skills.

The SEO Fix

Two tools:

SEO Tool #1: Start by using a WordPress plugin called Yoast. Use their free version. In this case, free works great. Yoast is a terrific tool for basic SEO needs. It's one of the few plugins I use.

This plugin is super intuitive and will begin to *demystify* SEO the moment you publish your very first blog post.

By default, just by using Yoast, you will easily start learning the basics of SEO.

As your post is written, Yoast will automatically begin creating a checklist of suggestions to improve your SEO ranking. Yoast uses a "red light to green light" grading system of your post which makes it super easy to understand and actually fun to play with. Learn more about Yoast at:
www.ewellsmith.com/Yoast

SEO Tool #2: The second tool I highly recommend is called SEM Rush. This may be one of the most

comprehensive SEO services currently available. SEM Rush keys in on every aspect of SEO from competitive analysis (perhaps my favorite part – it's fascinating to get a peak into other websites), **to keyword research which is incredibly important,** to backlinks, etc. SEM Rush can help you with the basics to even offering writing services to help build relevant content to more advanced services. To get a glimpse of the services offered, they let you test drive for free:
www.ewellsmith.com/SEMRush

You may be asking, "How long does SEO take to kick in?"

That's a great question and the short answer is: *too long*.

If you're waiting for SEO results, you may also be wondering, *how do people find me in the meantime*?

That's an excellent question too.

You need to promote your site. No other way of saying that. Otherwise, you will have what I call a billboard in the digital desert that no one sees as you start out.

Promoting your site comes down to the fundamentals. Start by doing this:

Have your personal email list ready when you launch – and send your post out to people who already know you. They will be curious to see what you're doing.

Since your personal email list is likely made up of close friends, family, and business associates, asking them a favor to forward your email may be helpful. Give them your "why story" briefly and let them know you could use their help. *I strongly suggest NOT overusing or abusing this ask for sure. In the past, I've made an effective ask and was pleasantly surprised at the reach as my original email was forwarded on.*

Email other influencers each time you create a post to let them know of your new post. In time you will find established bloggers that may want to share your content to their audiences.

If you already have personal social accounts set up (Facebook, Instagram, Twitter, YouTube, etc), leverage those to share your blog posts on. You can then determine what other social platforms you may want to engage.

If your goal is to build an income around your blog and you have products or services ready to share and sell, you can then explore paid ads. If your niche is dialed in tight, the beauty of paid search and paid social is you can laser target your audience by a variety of demographics. With Facebook, you can start with a very small dollar amount that fits your budget.

Getting people to your site is no doubt important. Getting them back a second and third time will depend on the value and consistency of your content to your targeted audience.

Yoast will pull back the covers on SEO quickly for you once you start posting with their plugin for free. SEM Rush will take you to the next level leveraging keywords to improve your organic ranking sooner than later.

At the end of the day, SEO is an ever-evolving, long-term, and incredibly important strategy. Again, don't stress out over this one, simply learn as you go and pace yourself.

Hobby Blogger Mistake #6

Overkill on Dark Design

I honestly thought my first freebie site looked so cool.

I used black for the background on the entire site! The font was white using tiny 10-point because I thought that looked cool too.

What I effectively did was make the readers eyes tired and quickly chased them off my site. Reading white print on dark backgrounds exhausts the reader's eyes quickly.

The Design Fix

Pay attention to mainstream media websites.

The primary dominate background is typically white on mainstream media news sites. It simply reads easier. The news sites will use dark backgrounds to emphasize a point here and there, but for the most part, it's a white background. It's just easier on the reader's eyes.

Now, the news sites will typically use a smaller font due to the volume of content on their home page. When you click on a link on the news site's home page, often times when you get to the story, the font size will increase some.

My suggestion regarding font size is we're not a news site with a staff of hundreds providing massive volumes of content daily. As a result, we have the space to use a larger font size. So let's do our readers a favor, making it easier for them to read our blog.

Hobby Blogger Mistake #7

Too Few Headlines on Posts

I had one headline on each of my posts on my first freebie hobby blog. That's it. The main headline.

That's an issue for the rest of the post. To the reader, it just looks like a lot of copy and there's nothing to capture the reader's attention past the headline.

The Headline Fix

We, as readers of other's blogs, don't read first.

We scan first.

As the reader, the way we know if a story is of interest or at least a part of the story is of interest is by the headlines throughout the story.

Here's a significant part of the strategy using headlines: If you were to view the headlines together as a long sentence, the headlines (disregarding any copy in between the headlines) ideally should tell a mini-story that pulls the reader down the page.

This will increase the chances of your readers reading the entire story, or at least hitting the important points you want to get across.

Hobby Blogger Mistake #8

Too Much Copy on a Page

Have you ever read a book that has no margins? Not likely.

Have you ever gone to a blog where the copy goes corner to corner to the sides of the page? It happens.

That's a problem because the reader feels overwhelmed. I made this mistake and packed my pages with copy on the black background. A double whammy. I'm certain I lost readers. No need for you to lose your readers.

The Copy Fix

Pretend you're writing a hardcover novel and need to leave margins.

Just like reading a physical book, we as readers want to have margins and white space. That makes it easier for us to concentrate while reading a screen.

You might notice something when you visit other top bloggers' sites. They typically have a lot of white space. The margins are often wide which helps the reader feel like they are moving down the page even faster.

Hobby Blogger Mistake #9

Outdated Theme

This may seem obvious but using an outdated theme is a common mistake for bloggers.

Many that already have a blog or website don't know if their theme is even working at the most basic level.

They look at their laptop screen thinking all is ok, yet fail to check to see if their blog theme looks and functions on a tablet or phone.

Today, it's still not uncommon to pull up a blog or website on a smart phone and see that the content and design present completely different than on a computer screen. Often times, it's nearly impossible to navigate an outdated theme on a phone.

The Theme Fix

Use a responsive theme.

Consumers are spending more and more hours every day on their smart phones and tablets than their laptops. The smart phone is the new TV. **The sale in many cases is in the palm of the consumer's hand.**

Use a theme that's responsive. I'm not just talking about themes that simply resize content to fit different screen sizes. That's what a basic responsive theme offers.

Use a theme where you can design each page (or your offer) differently based on content specific to laptop, tablet, or a smart phone. Use a theme where you have the option to include or not include specific elements of content that are seen on the PC and/or on the tablet and/or on a smart phone. Your content needs to be optimized for all devices.

Success at this point goes back to selecting a good tool like Thrive Themes.

Thrive Themes provides all those responsive options to further increase conversion rates, meeting the consumers where they are – regardless of whether they are using a laptop, tablet, or phone.

Hobby Blogger Mistake #10

Too Many Big Words. Too Many Long Sentences

We want to show people we're smart. Right?

It's our human nature. We do that by using big and fancy words when we speak or write.

You were likely taught in high school and/or college to write really long sentences with semicolons and commas to make a point. That all works fine if you're writing a thesis paper. Not so much on your blog.

The Grammar Fix

It's OK to break the rules.

Forget what your 12th grade high school English teacher taught you.

You want to write short sentences with simple words that people can easily read.

Popular blockbuster novels are written at the 7th grade level. *Time Magazine* is written at the sixth and seventh grade level. Most Americans read at the 7th or 8th grade level.

If you want to communicate well with your visitor, ***big words don't work well. Short words and short sentences work better.***

Hobby Blogger Mistake #11

Not Making a Clear Offer

Many blogs and websites are not clear on what they offer. The visitor shows up and leaves because the website does not offer a solution to a problem they have.

I never even made an ask of my visitors with my freebie blog. I had no offer. That's one extreme. I was a "hobby blogger" to the core. It's interesting to note that many larger corporations don't get this right either.

The "Make Your Offer Clear" Fix

Your reader needs to understand immediately what your blog is about.

Offer your lead magnet to pull the visitor into a dialog. You'll at least get an email address in return and then you can build a relationship and make additional offers. (re-read Chapter 5 regarding the Home Page)

Hobby Blogger Mistake # 12

Not Genuine. Not Authentic.

I can honestly say my first blog was not interesting at all to the reader. I did nothing to share who I was or what I was about. I was guarded, and I simply used the platform as an extension to my boring paper resume. We all know how exciting our resumes read.

The Authentic Fix

There's only one you.

One unique set of fingerprints. One unique personality. One unique set of skills. One unique voice.

You're already taken.

And others are taken too. Don't try to be someone else. Be you. Tell your own story. Own it.

The real reality of your life is interesting to people. **Share your real story. Be honest.**

People are more interested in your real life and how you overcome real challenges. Putting on a front is never effective long term.

Every single one of us has very real challenges. Sharing your vulnerabilities in a genuine way to serve your community will endear you to your community in a meaningful and impactful way. Transparency with your audience will do wonders.

Finally, allow yourself to share your passion for whatever service or product you will refer. **Let them know why you do what you do. People respond to energy.** The more authentic your energy is, the more interesting you will be to your audience. And if you have a creative bent, leverage your passion with your creativity.

Hobby Blogger Mistake #13

Trying to Be Perfect

Perfection is often the enemy of progress.

- If you're waiting for the right time to get started building your blog and for the stars to align, you may never actually get started.
- If you're waiting for your blog to be perfect, you may never launch it.
- If you're waiting to have all your content, you may never release it.
- If you're waiting to publish your first blog post because you keep editing it over and over and over, you may never publish it.

There's always a tweak to color, design, copy, and mechanics to be made on a blog. Always. Now this is the cool part...you can come back and make those changes any time you want. Just get started.

The fear of being perfect will paralyze you IF you allow it.

The Perfect Fix

Give yourself permission to NOT be perfect.

With that permission, you can take that first step of faith believing in yourself to blog.

You can launch your site when you think your blog's done, not perfect. (Your site, candidly, is never done.)

You can cut yourself some slack and know you're going to make mistakes.

You can know it's going to be ok. You learn from the mistakes and move forward.

You can know you're on your way.

Cutting yourself some slack allows you to enjoy the journey in this very moment we are in right now! Have fun with it!

Just get started and you'll begin to see what's possible!

***Note - It's Bloggable!* is the result of all the mistakes above and then some.** Interestingly enough, every one of these mistakes at some level disrupts the ability to establish deeper connections to impact lives and/or promote a product or service. You can easily avoid all of these common mistakes now.

"Affiliate marketing has made businesses millions and ordinary people millionaires."

Bo Bennett

Chapter Seven

Step 7. Understanding Affiliate Marketing and how you can earn money online.

A good friend of mine, John Rowley, is one of the very top affiliate marketers in the incredibly competitive health and fitness arena. His eBook, *Old School New Body*, was his first major digital success selling hundreds of thousands of copies.

For the past several years, John has been the one to constantly encourage me to transition from my hobby blogger mindset and start leveraging my blog as an affiliate marketing opportunity.

I've seen John's trajectory of success first-hand as his audience grew, reaching millions with millions of dollars in sales revenue coming in from across the globe. With his first eBook, I saw the hockey stick chart effect on his computer monitor at his office regarding his online sales in real time.

As I stated upfront in this book, success takes work. It takes effort. John by no means is an overnight success. He laid the groundwork. He showed up.

John is a normal guy who has worked very hard, overcoming several major life hurdles. He has spent a lifetime literally rebuilding his body from a life-altering car accident to owning the gym that the documentary Pumping Iron was filmed in with Arnold Schwarzenegger and Lou Ferrigno. I met John shortly after he lost everything in the real estate business in 2008.

Affiliate Marketing for Bloggers

As I was getting to know John, he let me know he was rebuilding his life once again, and that he was getting into affiliate marketing. I'd never heard the term. I didn't really understand what that meant. **Turns out there are a number of entry points into affiliate marketing.**

Regarding your blog, this is the unique thing about affiliate marketing: starting out, it's the fastest way for bloggers to get started earning passive online income. And it's very little risk. I'm still leading a trade association, serving loggers like I've done with fishermen, and affiliate marketing makes this possible for me to do this on the side.

Affiliate marketing eliminates the need to start with your own products or service to promote. At some point, you may want your own digital or physical products like John to share, but for now affiliate marketing on your blog is a proven income tool that many people have used while starting out. As you discover more about affiliate marketing, it only builds from there.

So, what exactly is Affiliate Marketing?

Sometimes I think affiliate marketing should simply be called "connection marketing" because that's exactly what it does – connects. As an affiliate marketer, here's my take of how this works:

> **You share a product or service you trust with others that provides a solution to a problem or need they have in return for a referral fee while leveraging your time.**

Is affiliate marketing easy?

No. Affiliate marketing takes effort. Like anything think else worthwhile, you will need to work at it. It will then work for you.

If you're looking for an easy road, affiliate marketing *is not for you*. Is it guaranteed income? No. **Can it be significant income? Yes**, if you're willing to put in the effort on the front end.

Let's leverage your time and build your POI

The one thing you and I and every human being has in common is that we all have 24 hours a day. Rich.

Poor. Healthy. Sick. Time ticks the same for each of us.

Most jobs or careers trade your time for dollars, capping your income potential. Affiliate marketing leverages your time and lifts the cap off of you. That has been proven over and over.

The more you master the art of affiliate marketing, the more affiliate marketing will return the favor of your time. And, all the while, you're being compensated for your efforts. You've seen me refer to it through ***It's Bloggable!*** **I call it building your Passive Online Income, your POI.**

Essentially, what you're doing is freeing up your time. **You are no longer trading time for dollars.** The better you master the art of affiliate marketing, the better your POI. And the more freedom you gain.

How passive in your passive online income?

Here's a candid look others may shy from telling you.

Even as you get your affiliate marketing machine going, building your POI, there is still work to be done. John would tell you that for sure.

There is no such thing as a fully 100% "passive business." If you own apartments that bring in a passive monthly income, you still need to manage the units in some form or another. You may manage a manager or serve as the manager making sure repairs are made, rents are collected, general maintenance is done, etc.

Just like owning apartments with a passive income, regarding your online passive income:

- You will need to monitor your affiliate programs to see what's working and what's not while they work for you 24/7.

- You will want to refine your marketing efforts for those affiliate programs working well for you. This will help you leverage your income and buy back more of your time.

What is an affiliate link?

Let's look at this in reverse.

If you've ever bought a book on Amazon that was recommended on a blog post you were reading, there's a very good possibility there was an affiliate link on the blog you clicked on to purchase that book.

A tracking tool you don't see called a "cookie" then followed you (from the link you clicked on) for a period of time. When you ultimately made a purchase on Amazon within the timeframe on the cookie, the cookie gave credit to the blogger who recommended that book to you. In return, the blogger making the recommendation was paid a small commission at no expense to you, in this case by Amazon, for the sale. And you got your book.

How does a "cookie" work?

Regarding the cookie, affiliate marketing programs may offer different timeframes for your visitor to actually make a purchase. For example, let's say the affiliate program you're promoting offers a 90-day cookie. If your buyer clicks on your link on your blog and doesn't buy product ABC right away, the cookie will then track your visitor the remainder of the 90 days left on the cookie. If your visitor then buys on day 53, the blogger, you, will still get credit for a sale for bringing a buyer to their site.

Important guidelines to get you going:

Do you tell your visitors you're using affiliate links? Yes. Be transparent.

That's the best policy to build trust. Do that upfront.

People respect an honest, transparent approach not to mention it's a legal requirement for a blog.

You may have noticed that I went a step further regarding affiliate links in this book. I also let the readers of this book know I use affiliate links for the same reasons I do on my blog.

Here's my Affiliate Disclaimer statement you will find my blog https://ewellsmith.com/Affiliate-Disclaimer. I want the reader of my blog to understand and clearly know that I get paid for the recommendation at no added expense to them.

How do you establish trust?

You've already started by letting them know you use affiliate links. Now do this one thing and you will be well on your way:

Think of your visitors as friends and family.

Would you share a product or service with your own family and friends you didn't trust?

Would you recommend a bad restaurant to them? Of course not.

Typically, we're proud to make a good recommendation. When it comes to restaurants, sometimes we'll give the person two or three of our top choices.

A good rule of thumb is if you don't know the product or service well enough to trust it, don't recommend it. Work with products or services you are proud to recommend, just like with your favorite restaurant.

How do you share a product or service you trust?

First, you simply share your story or experience with the product or service to your visitors in a friendly, professional, conversational way. Be honest with your feedback regarding the product or service. The good. The bad. The truth.

Second, you simply share an affiliate link to the product or service you trust, which will track sales back to you.

The companies that offer affiliate programs will provide a unique affiliate link for you to use on your blog that will track your passive referral income. It's a best practice to review the guidelines an affiliate program provides regarding the use of their links and the terms of their compensation programs.

Where do you find products or services to recommend?

Many of the services you will likely use to run your online business will offer an affiliate marketing link you can recommend to your audience.

You may be surprised how many companies provide affiliate programs. **Often times it's as easy as looking at the footer (the very bottom portion of the home page that indexes all the important links) of a company or blogger's website to see if they offer an affiliate program that you can help promote.** Once you start keeping an eye our for affiliate links, you may be surprised how many offer them.

I also suggest Googling "recurring affiliate programs." These are affiliate programs that don't just pay you for one sale, rather they pay you for ongoing sales as a product or service is renewed annually or billed monthly for example.

Along your blogging journey, you will discover other bloggers who have their own products and services like John Rowley to sell that are using affiliate platforms to further their reach and drive additional sales.

The #1 myth to avoid:

"I'm wasting my time sharing the same product I've seen on other blogs."

That statement is a myth. The internet marketplace is infinite.

Avoid the trap of assuming just because you know about a product or service that others do too. That's a huge myth.

I call it the "trade show syndrome" that many marketers start to believe. If you've ever worked a trade show and set up your booth, by year two and 23 shows later, you're sick of seeing your booth and think the design is dated. The reality is, it still may be very fresh, especially to the person who has never seen the booth the first time they walk up to visit with you.

Going back to my favorite analogy, how many of your friends and family know about your favorite new restaurant you found over a month ago? They may live in the same town you live in. They may have heard about it. It's also very possible they haven't. Unlike the town you live in, the internet is truly infinite with infinite opportunity to share your products and services.

Remember the blogging principle in Chapter Two, there's always a classroom of people behind you that you can help!

Wide-Open Opportunities for You

As a sidebar, just as I had no clue what affiliate marketing was a few years back, today I have to educate many in my trade association network how affiliate marketing actually works. When affiliate marketing comes up in person with my colleagues, they begin asking me questions out of curiosity. It's still totally new to most of them. That's despite the fact they have likely bought a product or service through an affiliate link. Again, opportunities are right in front of you.

Those opportunities to reach new audiences are there in most industries. The key is seeing the opportunities and leveraging them.

Three Last Tips

1. Leverage Your Efforts

You may also want to start interviewing the product owners, service providers, or book authors of those products and services you plan to share on your blog.

It’s an excellent way to network within the industry and find win-win situations to promote each other’s products or services. Flying solo will take much longer and the solo journey is not nearly as fulfilling and fun.

For your desired outcomes, always remember to leverage your efforts with others who share a common interest or goal.

As you establish more and more credibility with your blog, more opportunities will open up for you (some of which you may never dreamed of).

2. Thread the Needle When Possible

You can use the affiliate links, that you promote, on multiple posts. You can “thread the needle” across other posts or on your blog to further leverage the affiliate link for the product or service you are promoting.

Keep it relevant, meaning put the affiliate link in stories that relate somehow back to the product or service you are sharing.

3. Build Your “Resources Page”

Your Resources Page is valuable to your visitors. And it’s valuable to you as a passive income generator.
As you find affiliate products you use and trust to promote, create a Resources Page to share those tools with your community. I’ve visited others’ Resources Page to learn about the best products and services to use and this been incredibly helpful to me. So I’m doing the same and passing my

personal blog's **Resources Page** to you and my community. See https://ewellsmith.com/Resources

My intent is to provide *only highly relevant links in this eBook* to help you get started right away with your blog. There are other tools I use daily that I share on my blog's Resources Page that are also very helpful.

Once you set up your blog, you will want to set up your own Resources Page.

Remember, the "classroom of students" that's behind you also needs the right tools to get going just like you do. They will turn to you as their guide. Your visitors will be curious to learn the tools you use.

Perspective

I recently had a very interesting conversation with a young sales guy, 26 years old, who is helping me with my trade association.

I asked him which sales or inspirational books he likes in the sales space. As the conversation went deeper, I asked him if he liked Tony Robbins? He looked at me with a blank stare. He had no clue who Tony Robbins is. I was thinking, *Wow, the "classroom of students behind you" revelation I mentioned in Chapter Two is spot on.*

There's always an entire generation coming up that's behind you and I no matter what the age we are.

That's a cycle that will repeat itself for generations to come, leaving doors of opportunity open for all of us.

More Perspective

Think about this for a moment...

In my very large network of nonprofit organizations, over a 25-year span, I do not know a single person who has their own personal blog**. *Not one.***

In my social online network, which is in the thousands like so many today, I only know three or four people personally with their own blog. Again, opportunities to educate and share your knowledge are right in front of you.

"Wealth is the ability to fully experience life."

Henry David Thoreau

It's Bloggable! Book Bonus 1: The power of possibilities for you

Do you remember the excitement you had right before graduation? It doesn't matter if it was 8th grade graduation, high school, tech school, or college. Anticipation builds. What about the anticipation you had to get your driver's license? How about the thrill moving out of your parent's home? Moving into your first apartment? Or your first big move out of state? Overseas?

Do you remember the anticipation and the excitement that you felt during those special times of your life?

The **one thing, in one word,** the food bloggers have taught me that threads the needle between all the special moments in our lives (it's been all over this book in fact) is: **Possibilities!**

Possibilities and what you can do is what ***It's Bloggable!*** is all about.

By now you're probably realizing blogging is so much more than just blogging.

***It's Bloggable*! is not just about a blog but about how you can** achieve what you're after, with success and satisfaction.

Think about your blog as a metaphor for life. Some people have lived life grudgingly, just existing. Some have tried, failed, and quit. Others have tried, failed, but stayed focused on the possibilities and never gave up. Some have soared to great heights they never could have imagined as they leveraged and integrated their passion, opportunities, and skills.

Life is about the opportunities that are ahead of you. It's about using your purpose to impact the lives of others. It's about a brighter future for you, your family, and your friends.

There's something very special about the unknown journey ahead. It's a risk that energizes us.

I felt the same anticipation all over again as I was getting closer and closer to releasing my first book, ***It's Bloggable!***

Like with many people, I felt the nervousness that comes with launching into something new. In fact, a term we often use as bloggers and online entrepreneurs called, "imposter syndrome" became very real in this process with this book. I felt the fear of putting myself out there in a whole new way with this book. To be really candid, I was taken back by my own initial reaction to fictitious fears in my mind.

As I launch this book, I have no idea what surprises may lie ahead. One thing is 100% certain, however.

If I stop moving forward and stop using my voice to help others, opportunities and possibilities will never be realized.

Imagine if Colonel Sanders had listened to his own self-doubts or to his critics? Supposed he followed the path of many of those his age, 65 at the time, when he had the idea to start a chicken restaurant. Kentucky Fried Chicken would have never happened. Others his age were retiring as he was just getting started!

Your blogging journey is about to begin no matter your age. It's never too late. The good thing is, starting a blog is a whole lot simpler than starting a restaurant.

I'm excited for you. Remember to keep moving forward even if you're only taking one small step at a time. Before you know it, you'll be launching your own new journey. You'll start to realize just how impactful your voice is.

You just never know what opportunities will open up for you when you take a leap of faith. And that's exciting!

Let personal story be a positive driver in your life as you move forward. Let your voice be heard.

By now, you know that Hurricane Katrina and the catastrophic BP oil spill in the Gulf of Mexico impacted my view of, well, everything.

In New Orleans, we live our lives by **Pre-K and Post-K**. *K being Hurricane Katrina.* As challenging as Hurricane Katrina was on so many levels, she gave us the opportunity to create a whole new life. How we responded to the hurricane is what really mattered. The same applies to today's global crisis you and I and everyone have come to know as COVID-19.

For those who saw the opportunities to come out stronger, Katrina, for many, turned out to be a life-altering event for the better. For those that only saw the bad, well, they went down the path holding on to "*what was*" with an iron fist, complaining at every twist and turn.

Today, with COVID-19, we're facing new and surreal challenges none of us ever could have imagined. It's so important to know even the hardest moments in our lives can be an incredible turning point for the better.

How we choose to respond matters tremendously. I truly believe God reveals our greatest strengths at our weakest moments. And it's these strengths that help us see the possibilities moving forward.

Here's the bottom line: The possibilities of your past got you to where you are today but may not get you any further. Think about what's ahead and all the amazing opportunities. Many of them are based on your own, personal call to action.

The possibilities of your future are endless and what really matters from this point on.

A "sobering call" provided clarity to move forward

Five years after Hurricane Katrina hit the coastline, I received a phone call I will never forget. The call came about 45 days into the BP oil spill, a historic disaster I mentioned earlier in this book that polluted the Gulf of Mexico, releasing crude oil and methane gas into the water for 87 consecutive days.

The phone call I received was from a very well-known chef who called me to ask a very pointed and sobering question, "Will we have a fisheries left?"

I answered bluntly, "I don't know."

That gripping question from the celebrity chef has stood frozen in time for me to this day. I can still hear his voice as clear as a bell asking me that question. I can still hear my own voice in my mind today as I answered him, "I don't know."

I can still see my surroundings crystal clear while on that brief call. I was on a fishing dock in Venice, Louisiana overlooking the silhouettes of shrimp boats as the sun was slowly rising at 6:15 in the morning. The water was so still, not a ripple. It looked like glass, reflecting the boats.

That was my wake-up call!

All of our futures felt uncertain in that moment as fear was coming to a head with no end in sight. Fear seemed to rule the day for our commercial fishermen.

What we did know was this: based on our experiences overcoming Katrina, **how we think absolutely matters if we're going to make it out ok.**

Deep down we knew we had to keep pressing forward. We knew the BP oil well would be capped at some point. We hoped our fisheries would be ok. We knew the consumers across the globe would be afraid to eat our seafood. We knew the moment our seafood was deemed safe (our seafood became the most tested food source in the world), we would have a massive undertaken to rebuild the brands of Louisiana and Gulf Seafood. We knew we had to restore the consumers trust. We knew we faced the reality that we had lost 98% of our market. We knew this would take time. We knew we had to take this one day at a time. We knew we had to press forward.

After the chef's call, I literally had a poster made to keep my team on point to not only develop an Absolutely Mindset, but to maintain and keep an Absolutely Mindset.

I had these five words printed on that poster:

1. Positive
2. Possible
3. Faith
4. Action
5. Excellence

No cute acronym.

We had two copies of this poster printed. One hung on the wall in our office to be a constant reminder to our team and anyone who came into our office. The other poster traveled with us to meetings and was set in the middle of the room for all to see as a constant reminder.

I thought at one point, after seeing the poster for the first time on the wall, perhaps I should have put faith first on that list. The reality is that's not how it came to me following the chef's call. It just came to me.

I never questioned it to the point I would change it to make a cute acronym. I've kept it exactly how it came to me that day to keep moving forward. Let me lay out the progression of the five words and you'll see why.

In short, when we stay **positive** in the moment, we then have the ability to see the **possibilities**. When we see the possibilities (the keys to opportunities), we lean to our **faith** for a strength that takes us beyond our abilities that then commands us to take **action.** And, then, through our actions, we strive for **excellence**.

For me, praying is what activated the list. Praying was the action itself that put each of the words in motion.

There is no doubt in my mind we can come out stronger on the other side when faced with surreal challenges. I hope this book in this very moment in time we're all facing, right now, is **a "sobering call"** moment for you. Opportunities are all around you. Your voice matters now more than ever. Now, let's see what's possible for YOU as you move forward.

I personally want to congratulate you on finishing ***It's Bloggable!*** I also want to thank you for your time and for your commitment you gave to invest in yourself. As you just take one nugget of information from this book and start, you're on your way.

Before we go, and I want to ask you two favors.

First, I want to know how you're doing on your journey be it as a blogger or another amazing adventure. Please keep me posted on my private contact form only for those who read this book. Go https://ewellsmith.com/PrivateContact

Second, I want you to relax, enjoy your journey, and know your voice can make a difference. Your voice absolutely matters.

This is your time. Your purpose. Your life. Your freedom. All for you to enjoy at this very moment. Now.

Make it a great day!

P.S. If you felt ***It's Bloggable!*** was helpful, I've got one final favor to ask of you: please pay-it-forward and share with others.

P.P.S. I thought I was done writing this book. But I came back and added one more bonus for you on how I finally got my first book done after it sat for two years. If you've ever dreamed of writing a book or have one stuck in your mind or even have one on your hard drive collecting virtual dust, this next bonus is for you.

"Great is the art of beginning, but greater is the art of ending."

Henry Wadsworth Longfellow

It's Bloggable! Book Bonus 2: How you can finish and publish your book in just weeks.

I started writing ***It's Bloggable!*** two years ago, got writers block, and sat it down like a rookie not knowing how to press through. Like so many other frustrated authors, I'd written an unfinished book serving zero purpose and helping no one. My voice to serve you and others was silent. Something was missing. I figured out what was missing and I'll tell you what that was in just a moment. It became glaringly obvious and impossible to ignore. You will definitely relate.

Once my mind was made up to go forward and get this book done, not surprisingly, I learned a whole new set of skills that go with publishing a book that I was unaware of, one of which I knew was a problem for me. It's a problem every book author must face. In fact, it's a problem just about every entrepreneur will face.

One huge hurdle to overcome to finally get it done!

If you're dreaming about writing a book or you have an unfinished book like I had that bothers you to no end, I want to share with you **the most important thing** that I needed to do to get this book done.

I'll address the issue head on with you – and I'll give you the solution to help you which is stunningly simple.

This is the cool part for you: only those readers of ***It's Bloggable!*** *that have read this far will get that guidance.* ***You're invited to the PRIVATE page on my personal blog.***

Everything points back to your blog.

Candidly, I could tell you the answer in this book to close out the book on paper or in eBook format. However, I'm bringing you to my private page on my personal blog. I'm doing this to drive home the foundational principle I went over in the very first sentence of this book. *Everything points back to your blog.* **In this case, the book also points back to the blog.**

You see what I'm doing? I'm leveraging my book to bring you into my ecosystem online if I've failed to already get your there. I'm not trying to be tricky. I'm simply demonstrating a solid marketing tactic in real time. That's the beauty of a blog...it becomes your hub and spoke marketing and messaging tool to magnify your voice, increase your reach and grow your online community.

Join me using the link below to my private page to learn what totally propelled me forward to finally get ***It's Bloggable!*** done and the one thing I had to actually do to make that happen.

They say application of what you learn creates transformation. This process I went through proved that to be true so I could finally finish this book. You'll see it, you'll get it, and you'll want to do the same. It's hard to ignore once you accept it, and it will help ensure you get your book done too.

Here's your link to ***It's Bloggable!*** Book Bonus 2

If you're reading the eBook, simply click this link https://ewellsmith.com/BookBonus2 or if you're reading a hardcopy version of this book, type that link into your internet browser.

I'll see you there in just a second...

“Don’t ever, ever, not put out your voice. Keep sharing because you never know when a thought in your head that you didn’t put out was actually the thought that would change the world.”

Gary Vaynerchuk

Resources Recap

At the end of the day, or should I say at the end of the book, these three resources made it possible for me to blog with zero technical skills. The blog, in turn, inspired me to share and write this book.

Rock 1. www.ewellsmith.com/BlueHost

Rock 2. www.ewellsmith.com/Thrive

Rock 3. www.ewellsmith.com/GetResponse

Resources Page Online

Visit https://ewellsmith.com/Resources to see the other tools I trust and use on a daily basis for my blog and for my trade association work.

Editor

I want to give a shout out and thank you to my Editor, Jeremy Plaisance. His experience and expertise helped me to finish this book.

You can learn more about his services, which range from consulting to editing to assistance with web content and sales emails, by visiting:
www.411growthsolutions.com

www.ItsBloggable.com

It's Bloggable! Thank You

That's what we call the "Jenny" look after I've driven my wife a little crazy with my ideas. We now have a book to show for it! A final thanks to Jenny for sticking with me and to you too. We wish you the best on your blogging journey!

Reminder - don't miss your ***It's Bloggable!* Book Bonus 2**

https://ewellsmith.com/BookBonus2

“Don’t focus on having a great blog. Focus on producing a blog that’s great for your readers.”

Brian Clark

APPENDIX

Absolutely Mindset Podcast Interviews: Two successful bloggers who inspired my blogging and book journey.

Special thank you to Cassidy and Marla for sharing their voices with the world, serving others, and inspiring so many, including me. If you're a new blogger, or you've been blogging for a while, I believe you will enjoy and be inspired by both of these bloggers. Ewell Smith

Cassidy Tuttle

Marla Meridith

“Your email list is going to be your highest converting traffic funnel.”

Neil Patel

Cassidy Tuttle

How Blogging About Succulents Grew to a Six-Figure Income

After completing my very first book, ***It's Bloggable!,*** I wanted to surprise Cassidy Tuttle, the founder of the Succulents and Sunshine blog, whom I highlighted in Chapter Three. I reached out to let her know that after seeing her blog, the title of my book ***It's Bloggable!*** came to life in my mind. Her blog helped me realize just about anything's possible in just about any niche as long as you provide genuine value. I asked Cassidy if she would share some of her journey with you. Here's a snapshot from my **Absolutely Mindset Podcast** interview with Cassidy.

In the interview, after I explained to Cassidy how the name ***It's Bloggable!*** came about, she responded, "I love that. It's interesting. When I go to a bloggers' conference, people ask me what I blog about, and I say succulents. It's like they are waiting for me to say something else. I love how that idea came up 'It's Bloggable' because that's one of the things I love about this – everyone thinks it's super niche, which to an extent it definitely is. I like that it's something small and unusual that captures people's attention."

Cassidy then goes on to share her aha moment that started the transition from a photography blog to a succulent's blog. The Succulents and Sunshine blog was born on February 14, 2013.

"Those posts (about succulents) had been on my photography site for about a year. Then we redirected them all to Succulents and Sunshine and cleaned it up a little bit so we had the benefit of traffic from day one. That first year, we made about ten thousand dollars between ad revenue and an eBook toward the end of 2013. We were getting traffic and monetized the blog from the get go.

My goal was to help people trying to get succulents to grow in a less than ideal climates. I was living in Utah at the time where most succulents won't grow because it's so cold. That had been my angle from the beginning – less than ideal climates you can keep succulents alive in.

My goal was to help with that and for it to be a business too.

On the photography site, it was something for me to talk about, pretty pictures; but it definitely became a business at that point. I was never in it to do it as a hobby. I didn't think it would become a full-time income, but I did go into it with a mindset that this is a business."

Cassidy's Key Marketing Strategy from Start to Success

She says, "I was really just focused on organic growth in the beginning. SEO has always been my focus from the very beginning. I've had some shifts on how I feel solely focusing on SEO since then.

I really just started writing good articles based on what people were searching for and what I was able to answer, and just made sure the site was very search friendly.

We then started implementing great SEO principles, and we saw growth pretty quickly. Basically, every article we added, we were getting traffic quickly. That's changed a little bit. You can still rank in Google searches fairly quickly. I will say SEO was much easier in 2013, but it's still definitely worth pursuing now as well."

Cassidy's Book Deal Kept Her in The Game

In the next part of the interview, Cassidy shares how she, like every entrepreneur, has those moments questioning whether or not to stay in the business. As she was becoming recognized as the go-to-expert on succulents, book offers started coming her way. After turning down three offers, she explains how landing the "Idiot's Guide" publishing deal helped pave her path forward in her mind. There's no doubt that every step of a journey is about mindset. With two employees now, she's looking forward to what's next.

Cassidy's Marketing Snapshot Today – Full details in the podcast

- **SEO** – Today, 65% of the Succulents and Sunshine blog's traffic comes from organic search, which has been a strength since the start.

- **Email** – Cassidy has invested in email the past four years, building out several different email sequences and funnels. Her email campaigns take you on a journey that provides value along the way and ultimately ends in an ask for one of her paid products, which is sound practice. Here is how she achieves the success and how she diversifies her income streams.

- **Facebook vs ________** In listening to my conversation with Cassidy, you may pick up the same vibe regarding her Facebook efforts. She started a Facebook group that grew to 20,000 followers in the first year. As I type this, that number is now over 83,000 followers. Despite her group's rapid growth, I found it very interesting to learn the social media platform she's now focusing more of her marketing. She also shares how her Facebook group has helped her grow an email list.

You'll also learn how Cassidy integrates all of it together while leveraging the two assets she owns...her blog and her email list.

Cassidy's future involves a new product launch for 2021. It's a digital product for sure, and she gives our podcast audience the inside details...she's upping her game...tune in to the podcast.

If you've ever wanted to learn how to care for succulents, make sure to visit www.SucculentsandSunshine.com. Cassidy is the go-to-authority thanks to her blog.

This was just a snapshot. To hear my full **Absolutely Mindset Podcast** interview with Cassidy and a few final thoughts and tips she has for bloggers, visit https://ewellsmith.com/Cassidy

“People do not buy goods and services. They buy relations, stories, and magic.”

Seth Godin

Marla Meridith

How One Event Opened Up Opportunities to Work with Iconic Chefs

During my time leading the Louisiana Seafood Promotion and Marketing Board, Marla Meridith was one of a dozen food bloggers we flew to New Orleans following the BP Oil Spill disaster.

People were simply afraid to eat our seafood due to very real concerns. By the time the oil well was capped, eighty-seven days later, our fisherman lost 98% of their seafood markets globally. Billions of dollars in seafood sales evaporated. At the end of the day, it was our responsibility to creatively develop collaborations with many to rebuild lost seafood markets.

Hurricane Katrina knocked us to our knees in 2005. Along that surreal journey to recovery, we picked up a few invaluable skills that prepared us for the BP Oil Spill. PR and marketing were the tools we used following Katrina to rebuild lost markets then. Given the scale of the BP Oil Spill with over-the-top media coverage from around the world, we knew we would need to do things differently.

Working with food bloggers to help us tell our fishermen's story in a new way was one of the options on which we took a gamble. We called it the

Louisiana Seafood Food Bloggers Tour. It paid off. We will forever be grateful to the food bloggers who shared the fishermen's story to the world, helping to save an eight-generation history in this industry.

To say the least, interviewing Marla on the **Absolutely Mindset Podcast** was a ton of fun and enlightening. Here's a snapshot with Marla sharing how her blog came about.

The Invaluable Role of Marla's Parents

I asked Marla who or what inspired her from her past. I truly believe her response is so important to hear for any parent raising a child.

She said, "I'm grateful for how I grew up. My parents were always gracious, generous, and accepting of my creativity. I've always been sort of a creative, and they were always very nurturing of that creativity in my life. That perspective they had – to let me do what I needed to do to be that kind of wild artist – really encouraged my whole life. It was the footprint for what I am now."

Marla started her blog as a mom with a three-year-old and a six-year-old. She said, "My life was about packing lunch boxes every day, and I was training for marathons. I wanted to feed the kiddos as healthy as I could as little developing bodies. The blog started off as familyfreshcooking.com. Through the years, I've evolved and the blog's evolved. It's evolved into more of a lifestyle blog, which is what you see today with MarlaMeridith.com.

Marla takes you on her journey sharing how she got started. She refers to herself as the "Jill of all trades." To sharpen her skills, she's been very intentional attending bloggers' conferences with a focus on the creative workshops.

Marla Sets Her Own Schedule

Today, she still does it all; she edits her own videos, she takes her own photos, and she does her selfies and the fashion too. She'll tell you, **"I like to be on my own timing for things."**
Regarding the creative process, she goes on to say, "I love it all. I love every little part of it. I like that I can pivot. One day it might be the photography, one day styling something, or all of it combined."

How Some Very Cool Doors of Opportunity Open

We briefly discussed her trip to New Orleans with the food bloggers tour. I had no idea of the reciprocal impact of that trip. She inspired me to blog and the experience inspired her travels to Alpine villages across the globe, working with some of the very best chefs. More importantly, to this day, she still cherishes the long-term friendships with some of the other food bloggers she met while touring coastal Louisiana and visiting New Orleans.

Other Topics We Covered:

- What motivates Marla and keeps her going after twelve years of blogging.
- Why she was able to secure a book deal with a major book publisher. This occurred after passing up on two prior book deals she wondered if she should have taken.
- The three pieces that laid the foundation to monetize her blog.
- How she acknowledges the markets have shifted for food/lifestyle bloggers.
- How she looks at life today due to the craziness of the moment and leverages opportunities as they arise.

Perhaps the Most Important Question?

After looking through some of the recipes on her blog, I asked her why she included candy corn in her Melted Candy Corn Skillet Brownie recipe. Marla gave me a surprising and very candid answer. If you've got a sweet tooth like me, I've just given you good reason to search that recipe on her blog. It involves ice cream too.

Visit Marla at www.MarlaMeridith.com. Make sure to click on her Instagram icon to shop, and when you click the Pinterest icon, you can join her 600,000+ followers. (A lot of her blog traffic comes from there.)

This was just a snapshot. To hear my full **Absolutely Mindset Podcast** interview with Marla and a few final thoughts and tips she has for bloggers, visit: https://ewellsmith.com/Marla

Your Own *It's Bloggable!* Quote Page

What will your quote say after you've impacted peoples' lives sharing your voice?

"____"

Your Name: _______________

P.S. Share your quote with me…I'm really curious.
Let me know here:
https://ewellsmith.com/contact/

“Your Voice Absolutely Matters.”

Ewell Smith

Notes

Notes

Notes

Notes

Made in United States
Troutdale, OR
11/03/2026

56844510R00111